THE MAKING OF
CONGO

THE MAKING OF
CONGO

BY JODY DUNCAN AND JANINE POURROY

BALLANTINE BOOKS • NEW YORK

The photographers wish to thank the following for their assistance with this project:

Blake Londraville from the Eastman Exchange Team of Eastman Kodak's Motion Picture and Television Imaging Division; The Entertainment Technology Center; Fractal Design Painter; Adobe Photoshop; Apple Computer; Nikon.

Interior Design by Michaelis/Carpelis Design Assoc. Inc.

Photography credits: *For Paramount Pictures:* Merrick Morton and Barry Slobin. *For Industrial Light & Magic:* David Owen and Sean Casey.

Library of Congress Catalog Card Number: 94-96758

ISBN: 0-345-39358-9

Manufactured in the United States of America
First Edition: June 1995
10 9 8 7 6 5 4 3 2 1

Acknowledgments

We extend our gratitude to Frank Marshall, Kathleen Kennedy, Anne Marie Stein, and all of the talented people involved in the making of *Congo*. Thank you for making us a part of your family. Thanks, also, to our families at home—Jim, Jessica, Trevor, and Caitlin.

Jody Duncan
Janine Pourroy

Contents

Introduction

Published in 1980, *Congo* was a bestselling novel abundant with potential as a blockbuster film. Not only was it written by Michael Crichton—a respected and popular author whose books *The Andromeda Strain*, *The Great Train Robbery*, *Rising Sun*, *Disclosure*, and, most spectacularly, *Jurassic Park* had already been successfully translated to the screen—the novel was also richly endowed with elements that would portend a huge success at the box office: high adventure, danger and suspense, compelling villains, likable heroes, the promise of vast treasure, and the romance of a mythical city discovered within the heart of the jungle. Moreover, the story had as its central character a thoroughly charming mountain gorilla named Amy. *Congo* had it all.

Such remarkable potential did not go unnoticed by powerhouse filmmakers Kathleen Kennedy and Frank Marshall, who negotiated a deal with Paramount Pictures in early 1993 to

(l. to r.) Baird Steptoe, first assistant cameraman, "B" camera; P. Scott Sakamoto, "B" camera operator; Wayne Witherspoon, set production assistant.

Adaptations

transform Crichton's bestseller into a cinematic reality. What followed were two and a half years of preparation and dedicated, high-energy filmmaking. Massive soundstage sets that recalled the glory days of epic movie productions were designed and constructed. Exotic jungle locations were scouted and filmed. Authentic, utterly believable gorillas were created. The result— premiering Friday, June 9, 1995—was *Congo*, a Paramount Pictures release produced by the Kennedy/Marshall Company.

The film's release was a highly anticipated event, marking the latest offering from a filmmaking team that had been instrumental in the creation of some of the most successful and revered films of all time. Kennedy had produced *E.T. The Extra-Terrestrial* (1982), the highest-grossing film in motion picture history until it was edged out by *Jurassic Park* (1993), a landmark film also produced by Kennedy. Together, Kennedy and Marshall had an impressive list of credits that included *The Color Purple* (1985), the *Back to the Future* trilogy, *Empire of the Sun* (1987), *Who Framed Roger Rabbit?* (1988), and *Hook* (1991). They had also served as executive producers for the well-received animated features *An American Tail* and *Fievel Goes West.* In addition, Marshall had produced the popular and high-grossing "Indiana Jones" trilogy, while Kennedy was execu-

A section of the hieroglyphs carved into the interior temple walls.

J. Michael Riva, production designer (l.) and Allen Daviau, director of photography, consult on the setup of a shot during a jungle sequence.

tive producer for the 1993 Academy Award for Best Picture recipient *Schindler's List.* In 1991, Kennedy and Marshall stepped down from the running of Amblin Entertainment—the esteemed production company they had formed in 1981 with director Steven Spielberg—to form their own Kennedy/Marshall Company. With *Alive* (1993), the first production under the new Kennedy/Marshall banner, Marshall made his second successful foray into directing, the first being 1990's *Arachnophobia.*

It was during production of *Jurassic Park* that Kennedy engaged Michael Crichton in a conversation that would lead to the making of *Congo.* Producer Frank Yablans, who held the rights to Crichton's novel, was contacted and efforts to produce the film were immediately initiated. Legal technicalities were quickly dispatched and, in the end, Yablans was credited as executive producer, with Kennedy and Sam Mercer producing and Marshall directing. *Congo* was on its way.

Option

The movie opens, appropriately enough, in Africa with a breathtaking montage of stylized shots illustrating the sights and sounds of the continent. As the title sequence continues, a small scientific expedition from TraviCom, a high-tech communications company, is revealed climbing the steep slopes of Mount Mukenko, an active volcano in the heart of the jungle region once known as the Congo. The title sequence ends as the image

Early in the shooting schedule, director Frank Marshall (r.) admires an elegant hawk alighting on the arm of Mark Harden, the trainer.

of a glowing amber arch on the face of the volcano dissolves to a less imposing setting: a playroom in an American university where a 130-pound, adolescent mountain gorilla named Amy is revealed happily finger painting childlike images of her native jungle.

No ordinary gorilla, Amy has long been under the care and tutelage of Dr. Peter Elliot, a young primatologist who has taught her to communicate through American Sign Language. The achievement is made all the more remarkable by his employment of a sophisticated, computer-linked glove that translates Amy's finger spelling into the spoken word. With an impressive demonstration of Amy's computer-aided speech to a large group of colleagues and representatives from grants organizations, Project Amy is declared an unqualified success.

But all is not well within Amy's carefully structured and protected world. In recent months, the young gorilla has been experiencing frequent and terrible nightmares, and Elliot fears she is succumbing to the mental degeneration that often afflicts primates in captivity. Taking a cue from her finger paintings, Elliot surmises that Amy wants to go home, and he immediately begins to seek funding for an expedition to the Congo. One who hears his appeal is Herkermer Homolka, an enigmatic philanthropist with secret motives for financing the expedition. Having devoted much of his life to finding the lost city of Zinj—an ancient city that, according to legend, is surrounded by bountiful diamond mines—Homolka has recognized similarities between the symbol of an eye in Amy's paintings and the hieroglyphs reportedly found on the walls of Zinj. By funding and joining Elliot's expedition, Homolka hopes that Amy may at last lead him to the lost city.

Philanthropy plays no part in the motives behind TraviCom's expedition, however. Looking to secure a profitable jump on its competition, TraviCom has sent a party into the Congo in search of precious, chemically flawless diamonds that will take telecommunications into the next century. With an exuberant satellite transmission to project supervisor Dr. Karen Ross in Houston from expedition leader Charles Travis—the son of TraviCom founder, R. B. Travis—it appears that the expedition is a success and that the diamonds have been found. Within an hour, however, communications from the Congo are disrupted, and the TraviCom satellite feed, operated remotely from Houston, transmits a scene of devastation: The bodies of the expedition members, minus Charles, lie bloody and lifeless amidst the wreckage of their campsite. Another image is also briefly revealed on the TraviCom monitors—the blurred image of a strange and savage-looking apelike creature, species unknown.

Racing against his industrial competition, the elder Travis immediately orders a second foray into the Congo, commanding Ross to find and commandeer an expedition that has already been cleared to enter the region. A young and brilliant scientist who

Shooting one of the jungle exteriors, on location in Simi Valley, California.

Detailed drawings for the wall of the mural room, interior of the Zinj temple.

was previously engaged to Charles, Ross is intent on ascertaining his fate, and with no time to lose, she joins the Project Amy expedition. Leading Ross, Elliot, Homolka, Amy, and Project Amy colleague Richard into the jungle is Monroe Kelly, a well-educated, daring safari guide, familiar with the dangers of the jungle.

And the dangers are many. Upon its arrival in Africa, the group suffers a military attack on its chartered plane and is forced to make an emergency parachute jump into dense jungle. Braving innumerable overwhelming obstacles in the impenetrable Congolese rain forest, the expedition faces raging rivers and a deadly encounter with a ferocious hippo. Expectation builds as they climb Mukenko, nearing the vicinity of Amy's birthplace.

It is here that they discover the lost city of Zinj and the remains of the first doomed expedition.

In Zinj, the expedition contends with the greatest danger of all. Guarding the abandoned city and its precious mines is a vicious, mutant breed of gray gorilla, the descendants of a deadly security force trained centuries earlier by the people of Zinj. Using ingenuity and determination, the explorers battle for their lives against the brutal onslaught of the grays. Finally, under the heat and ash of the erupting volcano, the survivors annihilate the grays and make a daring hot-air balloon escape out of the Congo, leaving Zinj and its mother lode of diamonds forever buried beneath a layer of molten lava.

Tom Southwell, conceptual artist, working on the interior design for the Zinj temple.

Realizing such an ambitious story would require many months of planning and preparation before cameras could roll. Foremost on the minds of Frank Marshall and Kathleen Kennedy was the assembling of a first-rate production team. By the time preproduction was officially launched, Marshall and Kennedy had secured the services of director of photography Allen Daviau, a well-respected cinematographer who had photographed *E.T.* and *The Color Purple,* among many other films. Also brought on to the project was Anne V. Coates, an editor with a long line of impressive credits, including 1963's *Lawrence of Arabia,* for which she won her first Academy Award. Charged with bringing Frank Marshall's vision of the film to the screen was production designer J. Michael Riva, also a veteran of *The Color Purple.* Costume designer Marilyn Matthews, special effects supervisor Michael Lantieri, and visual effects supervisor Scott Farrar were also signed. Remarkably, all but one of the production department heads were multiple Academy Award nominees.

Also on the preproduction agenda were the design and development of Amy and the gray gorillas, a task that was undertaken by creature-effects ace Stan Winston and his Stan Winston Studio crew. Of particular concern was Amy. Creating an eight-year-old mountain gorilla of unquestionable authenticity would entail the utilization of advanced animatronics and the combined talents of trained performers and a team of skilled puppeteers. Similarly, a multitude of grays had to be designed and built and ultimately brought to life by a performance team. The training and choreography of Amy and all the grays, a process that would take several months, was the responsibility of primate choreographer Peter Elliott, a veteran of several movies featuring realistic ape characters. It was also during preproduction that Kennedy and Marshall commissioned a script from acclaimed playwright and screenwriter John Patrick Shanley. Shanley, who had scripted Frank Marshall's *Alive* and had served

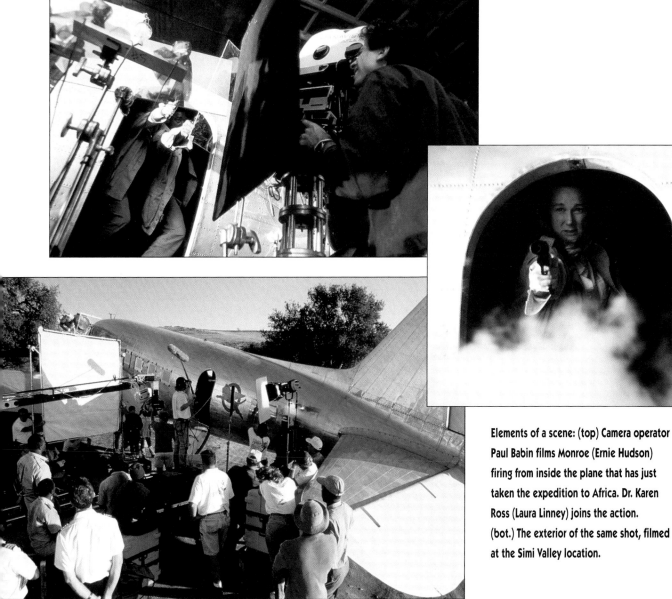

Elements of a scene: (top) Camera operator Paul Babin films Monroe (Ernie Hudson) firing from inside the plane that has just taken the expedition to Africa. Dr. Karen Ross (Laura Linney) joins the action. (bot.) The exterior of the same shot, filmed at the Simi Valley location.

Primate skulls present outside the ruins of Zinj, evidence that the grays attacked anything in their path, animal or human.

as both writer and director on Amblin's *Joe Versus the Volcano*, immediately began the process of translating Michael Crichton's bestseller into a suitable screenplay.

As preproduction continued, the lengthy process of casting both major and minor roles was initiated by casting director Mike Fenton. Cast as Peter Elliot was Dylan Walsh, a young actor who had previously appeared in *Betsy's Wedding*, *Where the Heart Is*, *Loverboy*, and as Paul Newman's son in *Nobody's Fool*. For the role of Karen Ross, Kennedy and Marshall chose Laura Linney. Linney's film work included *A Simple Twist of Fate*, *Dave*, *Searching for Bobby Fischer*, and *Lorenzo's Oil*. Linney also came to the project with considerable stage experience, having starred in stage productions of *The Seagull*, *Six Degrees of Separation*, and *Hedda Gabler*.

Expedition leader Monroe Kelly was to be played by veteran actor Ernie Hudson, whose earlier work included the "*Ghostbusters* films", *The Cowboy Way*, *The Crow*, *The Hand That Rocks the Cradle*, and *Speechless*. The mysterious Herkermer Homolka was a role assigned to Tim Curry. Curry had garnered much attention as the infamous Dr. Frank-N-Furter in the cult classic *The Rocky Horror Picture Show* and had gone on to play deliciously villainous roles in *Annie*, *The Three Musketeers*, *Legend*, and *The Shadow*, as well as starring as Mozart in Broadway's *Amadeus*. Rounding out the cast was Grant Heslov as Richard and Joe Don Baker as R. B. Travis.

After a year of preparation, principal photography for *Congo* commenced on September 26, 1994. What followed was just over four months of shooting in locations throughout Southern California and on soundstages at Sony Studios, as well as a three-week location shoot in the remote jungles of Costa Rica and second-unit filming in Africa. Wrapping in mid-February 1995, *Congo* entered its postproduction, during which time visual effects created by Industrial Light & Magic were completed and composited into the film. Additional postproduction tasks included editing, scoring, and the completion of a final sound mix.

The result of Kennedy/Marshall's unwavering efforts was a film reminiscent of the high-adventure movies Hollywood perfected in the thirties, forties, and fifties—movies such as *King Solomon's Mines*, *The Treasure of the Sierra Madre*, and *The African Queen*. In *Congo*, however, the romantic and old-fashioned sensibilities of those classic films were teamed with technology so new it teetered on a fence between reality and science fiction. Combining an epic style of storytelling, stunning visual images, and dazzling special effects, Congo was the kind of exciting film adventure audiences had come to expect from Kathleen Kennedy and Frank Marshall.

Kathleen Kennedy, producer

AUGUST 26, 1994

How did Kennedy/Marshall become involved in Congo?

Interestingly enough, Frank Marshall and I first came in contact with the project through Steven Spielberg. Both Steven and George Lucas were interested in it at one point—I even tried to talk them into revising the story so it would work as the third "Indiana Jones" movie. We toyed with that idea for a while and then abandoned it. But I never forgot about this project. Then, while I was making *Jurassic Park*, I spent time on the set talking to Michael Crichton. I asked him one day why *Congo* hadn't been made, and he said he didn't know. I decided to follow up on it. I called Frank Yablans, who still owned the rights to the book. Frank Marshall and I had a meeting with him and a few months later we put together a deal. We started preproduction in October of 1993. We knew we would need about a year's preparation on the picture. Prep time is the key to these kinds of movies.

Your original intent was to shoot much of the location work in Africa. Shortly into preproduction, however, the decision was made to shoot most of your exteriors in Costa Rica. What were the reasons behind that decision?

Initially, we had wanted to shoot locations in Burundi and Rwanda. A few movies had been made in Burundi, quite successfully. Our research revealed that it was an incredibly beautiful place, with an availability of trained technicians from South Africa and Kenya. We made various contacts and had declared that we were going to do our scout in Burundi when I picked up the newspaper and read that they'd had a coup and killed the president. Following that, everything began to escalate in Central Africa. We realized that going into Zaire, Rwanda, or Burundi—the region that used to be known as the Congo—was not going to be possible. Our alternative was Uganda, which faced the back side of the Virunga mountain range, the volcanic mountains referred to in the book. But in all honesty, that area didn't look right. Movies tend to give us a preconceived idea of what volcanoes look like. This mountain range is so old geologically that most of the volcanoes are no longer active, and they don't have the shape visually we expect them to. When we scouted Costa Rica, we discovered that the volcanoes there *looked* like movie volcanoes. Also, the Costa Rican volcanoes had jungle right up to their edges; whereas, in Uganda, the jungle actually stopped quite a bit short of the base of the volcanoes. It was important to the plot of our story—which included the discovery of a lost city—that we have thick vegetation at the base of Mount Mukenko. There were also budgetary reasons. There was an enormous cost difference between taking a full first unit over to Uganda versus Costa Rica. It takes only six hours to get to Costa Rica from Los Angeles, which was a significant advantage when it came to shipping equipment,

(l. to r.) Kathleen Kennedy, Frank Marshall, and singer Jimmy Buffett who portrays a pilot in the film.

et cetera. Logistically, Costa Rica was much more convenient than Africa. All of those considerations came into play, and we decided to shoot the majority of our location work in Costa Rica, with some second-unit work in Central Africa.

Michael Crichton's original story has been revised to some extent in the screenplay by John Patrick Shanley. Can you discuss some of those changes and why you felt they were necessary for the movie?

We tried to capture the most cinematic moments in Crichton's original story and explore them as fully as possible. We made some changes in terms of story and character that were relatively subtle. For example, the novel had a high-tech company looking for industrial-grade blue diamonds that would be used for military purposes. We developed that idea slightly from an emphasis on military use to an emphasis on the diamonds' potential for controlling communications and profit. We also added the character of Homolka, a treasure hunter who has been looking for the lost city of Zinj for a number of years. He is kind of a quirky character that we felt was needed—a character driven by greed who also serves to set up the legend surrounding Zinj. We also did a lot of thinking and planning for the grays' attack that comes at the climax of the movie. We wanted to create the effect of one long nightmare. Once the attack begins, the suspense and the terror continue to escalate, nonstop. Those were the kinds of revisions we made. Overall, the *essence* of what was in the novel is still in the movie.

In what way did you alter the relationships between the characters?

We changed the dynamic between Peter Elliot and Karen Ross at the beginning of the movie. Rather than having Karen take Peter and Amy along with her on her expedition, we establish that Peter has *already* begun his plans to take Amy home to the Congo. After the first TraviCom team is killed, Karen is so intent on getting into the Congo and finding out what happened to them that she accesses

on a sophisticated data computer anyone who has cleared visas into the Congo. She finds Peter Elliot's expedition and forces her way into it.

(l.) Kathleen Kennedy, director Frank Marshall (c.) and producer Sam Mercer consult during shooting of jungle exteriors. (r.) Checking the setup of the shot through the Panavision camera.

You've also changed the personalities and motivations of some of the main characters. The character of Karen, for example, is much more sympathetic than she was in the book. What was the rationale for changing her character?

We felt it was important that the audience like her and feel for her, so we've given Karen a rather personal agenda. We find out that Charles Travis—who is in the first doomed expedition—was her fiancé. One of the key reasons she insists on going in there is to find out if he is still alive. That gives her a nice emotional underpinning. We also suggest near the end of the movie that an emotional bond has formed between Karen and Peter and that there is the potential for romance.

This was obviously a huge production design project. What were the major design challenges going into this movie?

Our biggest concern was that there wasn't a detailed description in the book of the lost city of Zinj. We had to establish our own mythology: Why was Zinj there? How old was it? Who were the people that trained the grays?

Why are those people gone? Did the grays rise up and kill them? If they did, why? We had to answer all of those questions about Zinj before we could even *begin* designing it. Frank initiated brainstorming sessions which included myself, members of the art department, John Patrick Shanley, co-producer Sam Mercer, and a plethora of storyboard artists, and those sessions began to result in some exciting answers.

As you defined the city of Zinj, what were some of the major sets you determined would have to be built?

There was an entrance area guarded by statuary, a huge courtyard, a pavilion hall, the diamond mines, an adjacent geode room—basically, all of Zinj and its surrounding environs had to be built on the stages. In addition, because Zinj had to appear to be in the middle of a jungle, the design of the sets included the overgrowth of vegetation and a jungle canopy overhead.

According to the story, Zinj is located at the base of Mount Mukenko, an active volcano. How did the city's proximity to a volcano affect the production design?

It was a major consideration. Throughout the sets we incorporated the look of lava flows that have hardened and formed interesting shapes over many centuries. It gave the sets an unusual, spectacular look and also provided a rationale for why Zinj has been so difficult to find. We suggest that the city had been partially obliterated by these lava flows.

In addition to the production design, casting was a critical task that had to be addressed during preproduction. How did you and Frank Marshall approach the casting process?

We took the same approach to casting as we did on *Jurassic Park*. We wanted good, solid actors, but we wanted to let the movie be the star.

One of your principal characters was Amy. Did you ever consider using a real mountain gorilla to portray her?

The first thing we did was investigate whether or not there were any trained mountain gorillas in captivity, and the

Producer Sam Mercer and Kathleen Kennedy.

answer was no. There are lowland gorillas in captivity, of course—they are the gorillas you normally see in zoos—but we were advised very strongly not to try to use a lowland gorilla either. They are docile and very sweet, but they don't know their own strength. Then we looked very carefully at *Greystoke* and *Gorillas in the Mist*, and we realized that the majority of the work on those movies was done by combining animatronics with actors. It was early in the project when we gave up the idea of using a real gorilla and made the decision to go with animatronics. We brought in Peter Elliott to orchestrate the performances of the gorillas. Peter choreographed all of the ape sequences in *Greystoke* and *Gorillas in the Mist*, and he is extremely knowledgeable regarding simian movement and behavior. He told us we would need eight months to train the actors playing Amy, and six months for the grays. We went through an extensive casting procedure to find those actors. We brought in people who not only had athletic or gymnastic ability but also had some kind of dramatic experience. Performance and acting ability were very important in creating all the gorilla characters.

For Amy, the production had to create an authentic representation of a mountain gorilla. There was no reality on which to base the grays, however, since they are a fictional breed of gorilla. How did you and Frank Marshall envision the grays?

One of the things we decided to do with the grays was to give them a clublike hand. In the book, the grays pick up paddles to use as weapons. That worked as a literary device, but when you actually visualize them running with these paddles in their hands, it becomes a problem. So we came up with the idea that there have been many evolutionary strains of *Homo sapiens* that didn't necessarily evolve into man as we know him today. They evolved but then hit a dead end and died off. We're suggesting that these creatures are one of those dead ends or missing links. Our idea is that the people who lived in Zinj recognized a deformity of the hand in one of the gorillas and then inbred that among all the grays so that eventually they created a biological weapon—a killing machine. The grays have short, stubby fingers which allow them some gripping ability, but they have a wider, harder surface, which creates a powerful weapon.

You collaborated quite successfully with Stan Winston on
Jurassic Park, *for which he created a variety of animatronic dinosaurs. Was the Stan Winston Studio your first choice for the creation of the animatronic gorillas in* Congo?

Absolutely. We'd had a wonderful experience with Stan on *Jurassic Park*. In fact, we were still shooting *Jurassic* when we approached Stan about *Congo* and asked him to read the book. Fortunately, he found the project very appealing, and he agreed to create the gorillas, as well as an animatronic hippopotamus for a scene in which our characters are confronted by a hippo as they raft down a jungle river. The animatronic characters were crucial to this movie, and Stan has done a great job of realizing them.

On Jurassic Park, *Industrial Light & Magic created some wonderful computer-generated dinosaurs. Did you ever consider creating your gorillas through computer graphics?*

ILM will be doing some limited computer animation, but we knew from the beginning that we weren't going to try to do the gorillas with a lot of computer-generated effects. It is still very difficult to do hair and fur in computer graphics. Also, gorillas are very much like humans, so they are conducive to being portrayed by humans in suits in a way that dinosaurs are not. At least for now, computers and technology still cannot replicate the complexities of human movement.

What effects will ILM be providing for Congo, then?

They will create all of the volcano and earthquake effects. We will be shooting at Mt. Arenal in Costa Rica, which is considered one of the most active volcanoes in the world. ILM will support Arenal's volcanic activity with visual effects, creating the most realistic lava ever seen in a movie. The volcanic eruption of Mukenko and the ensuing earthquake which eventually destroys Zinj will require elaborate effects work from both ILM and special effects supervisor Michael Lantieri.

Kathleen Kennedy with *Daily Variety* columnist Army Archerd and director Frank Marshall.

Although the book was published fifteen years ago, it seems that this movie's time has come, especially considering the strides in technology that have occurred in the past decade. What are your thoughts on that?

When Michael Crichton wrote the book, he was really *ahead* of his time in many respects. The technology he was referencing in the seventies and eighties seemed like science fiction to some extent. High-tech devices such as phasic lasers and robotic, remote-controlled cameras didn't exist when the book was written but have now become a reality. Much of the technology was pure speculation on Michael's part, but as it turns out, it was very accurate, credible speculation.

CHAPTER·1

Jungle Book

Author/director Michael Crichton had just wrapped principal photography on *The Great Train Robbery* in England when he went to Hawaii for a short respite before the beginning of postproduction and promptly tore up one of his knees while bodysurfing. So badly was his knee injured that surgery was required, and Crichton had no choice but to postpone the completion of his film and return home to Los Angeles to recuperate. During this period of enforced inactivity, the usually industrious Crichton was left to sit on the beach with his leg in a cast and contemplate future book and movie projects.

Among the ideas that began to circulate in his mind was a story that centered on an ape that had been taught sign language—a premise inspired by the real-life Koko, a signing lowland gorilla that had graced more than one magazine cover by that summer of 1978. The story was nothing more than a vague notion when Crichton was asked to join Frank Yablans, then an independent producer at Twentieth Century Fox, for lunch. "Frank asked me what I wanted to do next," Crichton recalled, "and I said I had this idea for a modern-day *King Solomon's Mines* with high technology and signing apes. I said it just like that, in the most casual terms. We had a very nice lunch and I hobbled back to the beach." Two weeks later, Yablans called with the news that he had sold Crichton's idea to Fox. "I said, 'But I don't have an idea! All I have is *King Solomon's Mines*/high technology/signing gorillas.' And he said, 'Well, I've sold it.' "

Spending the greater part of 1979 writing the novel, Crichton devised a story line that dealt with a brilliant and driven scientist, Dr. Karen Ross, who joins forces with a primatologist and his signing gorilla to search for diamonds that will ensure military superiority for the government that secures them. A graduate of

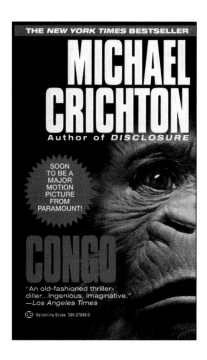

THE *NEW YORK TIMES* BESTSELLER

MICHAEL CRICHTON

Author of *DISCLOSURE*

SOON
TO BE A
MAJOR
MOTION
PICTURE
FROM
PARAMOUNT!

CONGO

"An old-fashioned thriller-
diller...Ingenious, imaginative."
—*Los Angeles Times*

Ballantine Books 345-37849-0

Harvard Medical School and an avid follower of all areas of science, Crichton infused this novel—as he had many of his previous stories—with mind-boggling technology. Although much of the technology in *Congo* was pure invention, some of it became reality even as Crichton was writing. "It was difficult to stay ahead of the technology. I would write these things and then everything I was inventing would turn out to be true. For example, I had written a long section about computers that use light instead of electricity—and then that was the lead article in the *Scientific American*, early seventy-nine. It was very difficult for me to get ahead of what was really happening with technology."

With the publication of the book, which immediately hit the bestseller lists, Crichton had fulfilled only the first part of the deal he had made with Yablans and Fox two years earlier. Now the time had come to adapt the novel to a film version, with Yablans producing and Crichton both directing and writing the screenplay. After completing a draft that was met with enthusiastic approval, Crichton and Yablans began researching locations for filming in Africa. They also began looking for their Amy. Learning that there were no trained gorillas available, the filmmakers made an offer to Koko herself. "We wrote to Penny Patterson, Koko's owner and trainer, and told her that we'd give Koko her own trailer and tutors, that we'd treat her like a child

Eddie Ventro (Joe Pantoliano) reviews the logistics of the expedition with Dr. Karen Ross (Laura Linney).

The expedition at the beginning of their journey into Africa.

star. And she wrote back and said, 'Koko can't do this. Koko is a big animal and is not accustomed to being around a lot of people.' So Koko was not an option. What were the alternatives? At that time Warners had just spent several million dollars on a test of mechanical animals for *Greystoke* and we managed to get ahold of that. Good as it was, I didn't think it was adequate for Amy. So I went to Fox and said, 'I don't think we can make this movie with mechanicals,' and that was the end of it. I wrote six scripts over as many years, from the late seventies to the middle eighties, but nobody ever made the movie."

The project that had seemed technically daunting in the early eighties was more than feasible by the time Kennedy/Marshall launched into preproduction in 1993. "There had been enormous advances in mechanical technology," said Crichton, "in terms of skin and textures and the amount of movement that

(l. to r.) Amy signs to Dr. Peter Elliot (Dylan Walsh) as Dr. Karen Ross looks on.

could be achieved through animatronics. And there was also digital technology to support and enhance that animatronic technology."

To draft a new screenplay, Kennedy and Marshall contacted New York–based screenwriter John Patrick Shanley and arranged a meeting in Los Angeles. "I sat down with Frank, Kathleen, and the art department," Shanley recalled, "and we went through everything. Essentially, they were already in pre-production. They had developed the gray gorillas and the art department had photographs of different locations that they could use to shoot the various scenes in the book. I went through my ideas for the film, using the visual aids that the art department had plastered all over the room. At the end of that meeting, it was clear that I was going to write the movie."

Shanley carefully examined the book to determine which elements would translate well to film and which would not. "I looked for all the elements that I thought were interesting, things like a guy and his talking gorilla, the lost city, the search for diamonds, the high-tech company, et cetera. And then I thought about everything that was going on in Central Africa, realizing that all of that was going to have to be acknowledged to some degree. We *had* to acknowledge that there were things that had gone on in Africa since the Tarzan movies were made." Shanley also looked for ways to update the story in regard to the technology. "Technology had changed radically since the book was written," Shanley noted. "Amy's proficiency with American Sign Language, for instance, may have been very much the news of the day back when Michael Crichton originally wrote the novel, but now we've all seen numerous examples of primates who have learned communication techniques. I wanted to do something we hadn't seen before and to find a way to bring this topic into the next decade. It occurred to me that developments in virtual reality would lend themselves to having Amy actually be able to talk in the film through sensors that could read her body language and translate them into audio. I didn't know it when I came up with the idea, but that technology actually exists. I soon discovered that whatever you can imagine is already being done."

Another element requiring updating was the search for rare diamonds that, in the book, motivates Ross's expedition into the Congo. Crichton had explained the value of the diamonds in terms of their potential use for high-tech military weaponry. For

Homolka (Tim Curry) explains the limitations of his financing for the expedition.

a post–Cold War movie, however, a different rationale was required. "It seemed to me that telecommunications is what the next ten years will be about," Shanley commented. "And, to me, communication was very much what the book was about—communication between Amy and Peter and the communications going on within Karen's company. I liked the idea of making the diamonds essential to the development of telecommunications."

In addition to updating some of the technology in the book, Shanley looked for ways in which to flesh out the main characters. No character went through more of a transformation from book to screenplay than Karen Ross. The ruthless young woman of Crichton's book was humanized in Shanley's screenplay. "I gave Karen the back story of having been in the CIA," Shanley explained. "She was incredibly good at it, but in the end she left because they were a loveless bunch of sons of bitches, as she says in the script. So she goes into the private sector, thinking that it is going to be different there. But she soon begins to suspect that it is the same story at TraviCom. Human life is put second to technology and the pursuit of filthy lucre. So she is someone who is very capable but also determined not to lose her humanity. And she is on this expedition, in part, to look for someone she once loved. I thought that was much more inter-

In Africa, the expedition is detained by the local militia.

esting. It also explains her attraction to Peter Elliot. He is a teacher and very unlike the people she normally deals with. He is in the Congo, not from greed but out of love and concern for Amy. He is something of an innocent, and that makes him very attractive to Karen."

A character not featured in the book but created for the film was Herkermer Homolka, a self-serving character with a mysterious background who funds the Project Amy expedition in hopes of finding the lost city of Zinj and its fabled diamond mines. "I thought it was important that there be someone in the group whose motives were not clear and who was up to no good," Shanley commented. "If everyone on the expedition was noble and motivated by the same thing, that would have lacked interest. Homolka is also the person who knows about the lost city, and through him I was able to provide the script with all of the exposition and background of Zinj."

Although by his own admission Shanley was no authority on the subject of Africa when he embarked on the *Congo* project, he was something of an expert on gorilla behavior and was thus well prepared to write the character of Amy. "I've been studying gorillas for years. It started back when I was writing a comedy about different kinds of gorillas and apes that were going to be

(top) Expedition arrives at landing strip in Africa.

(top) Monroe (Ernie Hudson) and Karen on alert in the ruins of Zinj.
(bot.) Kahega (Walé) and Monroe speaking to a Mizumu warrior.

played by people. I felt I should find out about their physicality and their behavior, so I went to zoos and sat with gorillas for hours. I also read all the books by people who have observed them in the wild. I was able to bring all of that research to *Congo*. Gorillas are so compelling and so like people; and yet, because they are animals, they are inexplicable."

In contrast to Amy's lovable, childlike character, the grays were conceived as monstrous freaks of nature. "When I went into the first meeting with Frank and the art department, I said, 'These animals have got to be diseased; they have to have tumors and open sores. The news for them has to be very bad. It has to be clear that this is not a species that is going to thrive and that there is something terribly wrong with it—it is not a normal species of animal. They had to be, as Peter says, 'a genetic dead end.' There are certain animals that are just killing machines, and so you have no qualms about killing them. The grays are that—insane killing machines."

In the end, John Patrick Shanley created a screenplay that was, at its heart, the kind of old-fashioned adventure that Michael Crichton had originally envisioned while sitting on a Southern California beach with his leg in a cast. "I tried to build a bridge between the old and the new," Shanley commented, "and I tried to elevate the humanistic elements of the story. It is difficult to write these kinds of adventures now that every corner of the earth has been fully explored. But the one place that is endlessly surprising is that place inside a human being."

A gray attack in the mine.

October 4, 1994 / San Bernardino, CA

The day was supposed to be a scorcher. Just days before the production unit's arrival, the city of San Bernardino, situated some seventy miles east of Los Angeles, was still in the grip of a heat wave that had been blazing since early July. But now, temperatures reaching well over one hundred had suddenly given way to a dank chill, and the desert sun, which the company had counted on to suggest the hot sun of Central Africa, had disappeared behind a dark cloud cover.

The company had come to San Bernardino to take advantage of the airstrip at Norton Air Force Base, once a thriving military outpost but now a casualty of recent base closures throughout California. As a stand-in for a Central African airport, Norton was ideal. It sat within an arid terrain that was geographically similar to the Central African landscape, and, built in the early forties, the base was devoid of ultramodern buildings. The only necessary set dressings had been a few strategically placed backdrops, several dilapidated false fronts, and fabricated palm trees scattered here and there.

It is only seven days into production and the company is clipping along at a good pace, despite the bitter cold. Slated to be filmed today are shots of Homolka, Elliot, Ross, and Amy deplaning from their chartered 727 as they arrive in Africa and their meeting with guide Monroe Kelly and safari liaison Eddie Ventro. To complete a scene of dialogue between the major characters aboard an airport vehicle, the actors spend most of the day circling the airstrip in an electric cart that is hitched to a specialized truck equipped with

cameras and lights. Positioned on the truck are Frank Marshall, director of photography Allen Daviau, and first assistant director Katterli Frauenfelder. Sitting a safe distance from the cast and crew is a Mercedes-Benz rigged to explode by the special effects crew for a shot in which a bomb is detonated in the car of the unnamed African government's president. Dozens of extras dressed as members of a Central African militia lend an ominous tone.

Wearing heavy coats and gloves, crew members huddle together in an airplane hangar that provides only cold and drafty shelter. Waiting for each new setup, actors warm their hands with cups of hot chocolate and coffee and enjoy the temporary comfort of jackets and mufflers before stripping down to safari wardrobes of shorts and lightweight shirts as they are called back to shoot yet another take on the electric cart. The actors gamely ignore their gooseflesh as they are spritzed with glycerin by the makeup crew to simulate perspiration.

Marshall and his crew prepare to shoot the group as it leaves the 727 parked on the ramp. Conversation dies as crew members turn their attention to the plane to witness the expedition's arrival in Africa. One by one, the cast members disembark. All is going well. Suddenly, Amy emerges from the plane and chaos ensues. The two normally docile golden retrievers belonging to Marshall and Kathleen Kennedy quickly rise, threatened by the presence of a seemingly real mountain gorilla. The dogs bark furiously, straining at their leashes. Startled by the dogs' response, Lorene Noh, the actress performing as Amy, retreats in fear. Kennedy struggles to restrain the agitated dogs. It is an unexpected canine testimonial to the verisimilitude of Amy. Stan Winston and his crew, who have labored for months to create her, exchange delighted smiles.

CHAPTER·2

Defining Zinj

Creating a visual backdrop for a film that included a mythical lost city, uninhabited acres of jungle, and a violently erupting volcano would clearly be a vital concern during *Congo*'s preproduction. The overall look of the film—in essence, everything the audience would see on-screen—had to be conceived and illustrated before anything could be realized. Kathleen Kennedy and Frank Marshall knew the production design for *Congo* was no ordinary assignment and turned immediately to production designer J. Michael Riva, with whom they had collaborated on *The Color Purple* in 1985. A veteran of the film industry, Riva had served as production designer for films as diverse as *Ordinary People, Lethal Weapon 1* and *2, A Few Good Men, Radio Flyer, Dave,* and *North.*

Riva approached *Congo* with characteristic enthusiasm, officially setting up shop for the art department in January 1994 at Raleigh Studios in Hollywood, situated close to the Paramount

(facing pg.) Last painting of mine area, from top of long stairway [Cranham].
(l.) Early pavilion sketch, as entrance to tomb [Cranham].
(r.) Sketch for gargoyle [Johnson].

(top) Carol Kiefer, art department coordinator, and J. Michael Riva, production designer.
(l.) Preliminary sketch for interior pavilion statue. Early sketch for back wall of gate, showing multiple levels for easy gorilla movement [Johnson].
(r.) Early sketch of tomb room [Johnson].

lot. Carol Keifer was hired as art department coordinator, with the responsibility of establishing the office and managing the department throughout the design and construction processes. Assisting Riva with the tremendous load of research the movie would require was Deborah Roth, who helped compile and sort through volumes of reference materials. Storyboard artist Steve Lyons had begun working with Frank Marshall on some initial renderings based on Crichton's novel six weeks prior to preproduction, and veteran artist Sherman Labby took on storyboard-

ing duties when he joined the design team in January.

By February the art department had begun assembling the artists and designers who would transform nebulous thought into concrete reality. Illustrators Jack Johnson and Tom Cranham were hired to render preliminary sketches; Tom Southwell signed on as conceptual artist and computer graphics designer to work out the hieroglyphics for the walls of the lost city and to create the film's logo. "The artists were essential in developing the look for the film," Riva noted. "We had lunch meetings with Frank where we would exchange ideas—we called them the 'think tank lunches.' Everyone would throw ideas around. It was a very creative and rewarding process, and it helped define the visual concepts for the film."

First on the art department's agenda was exhaustive research that would guide the filmmakers as they developed designs for the mythical city of Zinj. "Frank wanted Zinj to be as dramatic and dynamic as possible," Riva commented. "He wanted it to look as if it had come out of an ancient culture and had been sitting there in the jungle for two or three thousand years. In order to do that, we went back as far as we could in our research, to prehistoric times, and started reading about the evolution of humans and the entire history of humankind. We followed mankind through all its vari-

(l. to r.) Jack Johnson, illustrator; Charles Daboub, set designer.
(below) Paint sketch for Monroe's truck [Cranham].

MUNRO'S TRUCK

(top) Robert Fechtman, set designer.
(bot.) Projection sketch past heads and
ziggurat to pavilion [Johnson].

ous migrations up from Central Africa, through Arabia, and into Europe and Asia. The thing we found most interesting was that the primitive cultures were very similar. We began to see a common link in the art and architecture of these early cultures."

Research into the physiology and behavior of gorillas was also initiated under the guidance of Charles Horton of Zoo Atlanta, who came on board the *Congo* project as a consultant. Although the design and construction of Amy and the gray gorillas would be the responsibility of Stan Winston, the art department had to come to a solid understanding of simian behavior as well. "In our research," Riva said, "we learned that the behavior of apes— whether they are chimpanzees, gorillas, or baboons—is dictated by their environment. Gorillas are very peaceful animals because they live in the mountains where food and water are plentiful. Chimpanzees, on the other hand, live in a harsher environment, which has forced them to evolve into a much more aggressive animal. We discovered a similar principle in the evolution of human civilization: In both ape and human societies, deprivation, or need, caused major sociological changes. It was an interesting lesson that helped us to understand another aspect of the

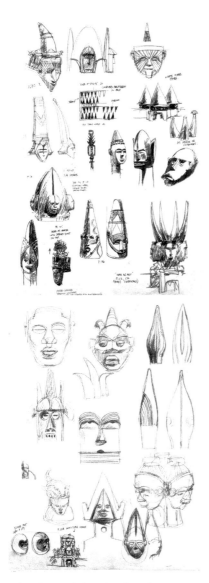

"CONGO"
CITY OF ZINJ

(previous pg.) Final elevation of stone heads above Zinj gate. Concept studies for gate heads [Johnson].

(l.) Early head studies for gate, sculpture, etc. [Johnson].

(r.) Map of Zinj from first camp to volcano [Johnson].

Congo story. In *Congo*, humans and apes came together when one society needed the other. The people of Zinj needed the grays to guard their mines, so they trained them to be an aggressive security force, which was the antithesis of what they naturally wanted to be."

All of the research enabled the filmmakers to begin assembling a logical mythology for the city of Zinj and the ancient

(l.) **Projection sketch for geode end of mine [Johnson].**

(r.) **Four early studies of mine area [Cranham].**

culture from which it had evolved—a mythology that would guide them not only in the development of the story but also in the conceptualization of the Zinj sets. As conceived by Marshall, Kennedy, screenwriter John Patrick Shanley, and the design team, Zinj was the product of a great mining colony that had been established in the name of an Egyptian pharaoh sometime around 1500 B.C. Exploring the possible consequences of generations of excessive wealth on such a society, the filmmakers considered the declines of Sodom and Gomorrah, which led them to another biblical connection—Solomon and Sheba. Separately, the design team had come full circle to Michael Crichton's initial notion of a story that had something to do with King Solomon's mines. "We kept building this story about a mine that belonged to a pharaoh's daughter," Riva explained. "In our scenario, the pharaoh's daughter married Solomon, and Solomon then owned the mines of Zinj. The city became bigger and bigger and that's when the society started to degrade."

Drawing upon their research and the invented back story of the mines, the designers presented Marshall with a look for Zinj that was at once nonspecific and familiar. "There was a lot of influence from Egypt," Riva said, "primarily in the heads and the statuary. But the city also had a lot of home-grown architecture that tapped into the African source. Some of the architectural design was reminiscent of Great Zimbabwe, which was probably the only large city built of rocks in Africa. We really

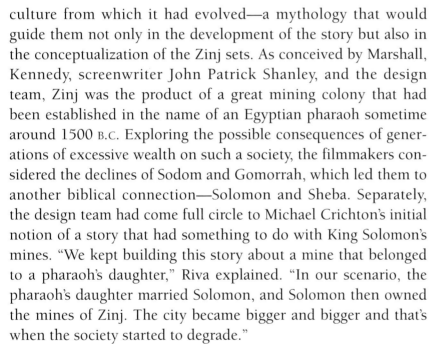

wanted, more than anything else, for the architecture to reflect the elements of *many* different societies. We wanted the audience to look at this city and think they see a little Egyptian influence, a little Mayan influence, even a little Cambodian influence. The whole city was a mystery for hundreds and thousands of years, and we wanted to retain that feeling of mystery in the sets. When we get to the end of the movie, we still don't know much about the people who lived there."

While the architectural designs were influenced by a multi-

(l.) **Study for long stairway into mine [Cranham].**

(r.) **Mine and catacomb sketch [Cranham].**

(bot.) **Early painting of mine [Cranham].**

tude of cultures, including native African, logic demanded that the building materials reflect what would have been readily available to the people of Zinj. For that reason, Riva limited the colors and textures of the city to those actually found in that region of the African jungle. Located at the base of a volcano, Zinj was made to look as if it had been built primarily of red and black volcanic rock.

At this point in preproduction, many of the sets that would comprise the city of Zinj were firmly established designs; others would not be clearly defined until the script had been finalized. "We proposed to Frank that there be a front gate guarded by three large stone heads where the expedition would enter a pavilion," recalled Riva, "but we were still unclear as to what would happen to our characters once they got *inside* the city. It could be anything we wanted it to be. Eventually we came up with the idea of a central corridor beyond the entrance for the characters to pass through as they walked toward the pavilion. Frank also thought there should be a certain exploration and

wandering through this *incredible* place—as opposed to entering Zinj and being inside for the rest of the movie. So we devised this big football field courtyard outside the pavilion that we were able to use toward the action of the story." Final designs also included a mine set and an adjacent geode room where the characters discover a "geological heart of diamond."

In developing *Congo*'s production design, Kennedy, Marshall, and Riva drew on the African experience they had shared while making *The Color Purple* years earlier. At the completion of principal photography for that film, the trio had gone to Africa to

(previous pg.) Early conceptual painting of Zinj wall, gate, and courtyard; sketches for gargoyles [Johnson].

(above) Completed Zinj column.

(middle) First sketch of Zinj and camp area [Johnson].

(bot.) Early sketch for Zinj gate [Johnson].

shoot second-unit footage. It was a memorable experience for all concerned. "Kathy, Frank, and I were together in Africa for almost three weeks, so we had a collective memory of it," Riva said. "We began to pool our knowledge and our remembrances and tried to include at least the *flavor* of those memories in the designs. Most of all, we hoped we could convey our wonder of Africa and how beautiful it is." This shared vision naturally led the filmmakers to Africa as their first choice for location shooting, and they made several return trips to scout sites. Eventually, however, the political instability of the region and the tremendous cost of transporting cast and crew led Kennedy and Marshall to the decision to limit the African shoot to a wildlife unit.

(top) Early conceptual drawings for Zinj.
(bot.) Construction blueprint for Zinj gates.

Sketch of mine area with waterfall
[Cranham].

While Marshall had intended from the beginning to erect the sets for Zinj on soundstages where conditions such as lighting and climate could be better controlled, it was now apparent that he would have to come up with creative alternatives to Africa for other locations as well. After several possible sites were scouted—including Chiapas, Mexico, where a revolt was in progress—it was decided to film many of the exteriors in Costa Rica, where location manager Paul Pav had discovered a number of phenomenal sites bearing active volcanoes and lush jungle that closely resembled Africa's rain forest. For exterior scenes requiring the look of the continent's arid savannas and plains,

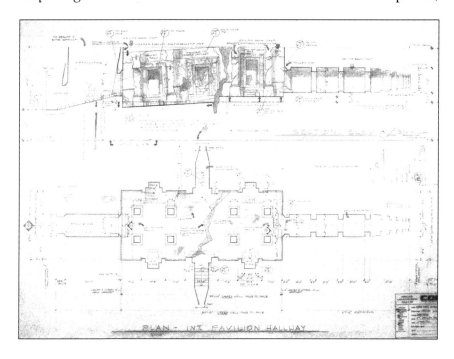

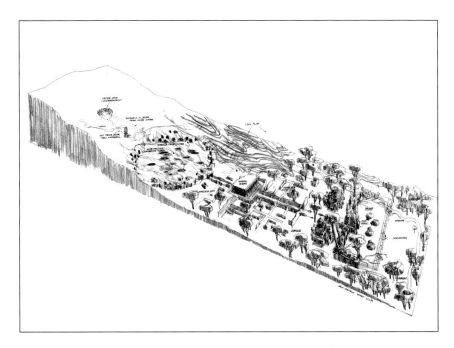

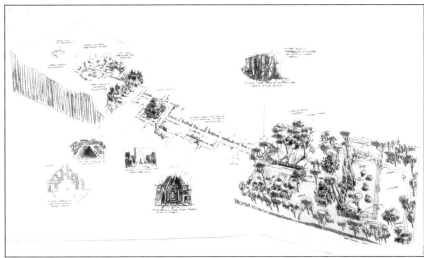

(top, middle) Volume maps of Zinj from first clearing, gate, maze, mural room, mine, and geode [Johnson].
(bot.) Interior, pavilion hallway plan, and elevation [Fechtman].

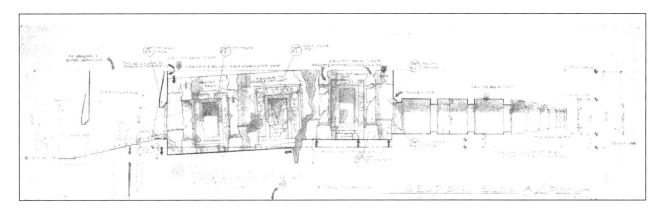

(l.) One of the decorative stone monkeys outside the Zinj temple;
(r.) Gorilla and gorilla/man studies for statuary and architecture [Johnson].

Pav and assistant location manager Debbie Page uncovered locations in and around Southern California that could unquestionably double for Africa.

As Marshall and the art department refined the overall look of Zinj—with sketch upon sketch reflecting the ever-evolving concepts—they also began considering logistical concerns in the physical layout of the sets. It was decided to construct the city of Zinj on two large soundstages at Sony Studios. The mammoth Stage 15—which had once been home to the Yellow Brick Road of MGM's beloved 1939 classic *The Wizard of Oz*—measured 311 feet in length and 40 feet from the stage floor to the permanent fixtures above, while Stage 30 offered a 50-foot ceiling and a 130-by-237-foot space.

To determine the dimensions and layouts of specific sets, illustrator Jack Johnson created a series of composite sketches that showed the various sections of the city. These sketches served as maps for the filmmakers. "I came up with some studies to help visualize possible caves, entrances, tunnels, architecture, and so on," Johnson noted. "Those studies helped us to see how things would look and fit in the stage area we had available. They also showed a clear order and helped keep things in perspective. I did thirty or forty of these composites as the story

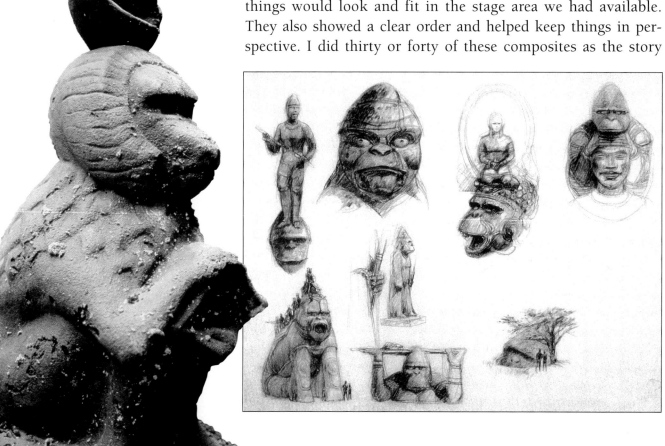

Mine and catacomb sketch [Cranham].

developed. They created a common understanding of what was going on within the film and what would make sense visually." Johnson created two different kinds of maps. One showed the slightly raised front view known as an elevation that illustrated the various sections of the city as they would appear if the camera was facing the set. The other kind of map was drawn from an overhead perspective and looked like a series of small, rectangular, single-frame storyboards linked together in numerical order.

In addition to the stage space considerations, the accommodation of special effects had to be incorporated into the architectural plans of the buildings. Because the story called for an enormous earthquake and volcanic eruption to level the city at the end of the film, the massive Zinj sets had to be stable and strong enough to serve as a stage area during filming, yet rigged in such a way that they could be made to shake and collapse on cue. Similarly, the pavilion would be equipped with a sinkhole, while the geode room would be built in such a way that it could be made to crack and split in half. Riva and special effects supervisor Michael Lantieri met to discuss the structural requisites and ultimately determined that the Zinj sets would have to be built on a platform above the stage floor to facilitate the special effects rigging.

Aiding the design of such complicated sets were three-dimensional foam models. Assistant art director Robert Woodruff joined the design team in March and began building the models out of a soft, nontoxic Styrofoam, similar to the material used in floral arrangements. "I cut the Styrofoam into a basic shape and

(l.) Final sketch for the Zinj wall and gate [Johnson]; (top) Sketch for the approach to Zinj [Johnson]; (r.) View from inside Zinj gate towards pavilion [Johnson]

then finessed it by hand," Woodruff explained. "I built models of several different sets to help show the relationship of the structures to each other. The model of the mining area was made out of clay, however, because it continued to change quite a bit. It made more sense to keep it as a free-form shape." The models were helpful in determining which areas would fall during the earthquake, while providing a better visual grounding for the filmmakers and set builders.

By late spring, art director Richard Holland and assistant art director Wendy Mickell had been brought on board, along with set designers Charles Daboub, Gary Diamond, Robert Fechtman, Sally Thornton, and Darrell Wight. "My main function was to be a right hand to Michael Riva," explained Holland,

"to coordinate the art department and make sure we were all going in the same focused direction. I helped push things ahead in more practical terms—getting going on drawings, models, plans, elevations, and so on." Once final designs were approved by Frank Marshall, the set designers translated those concepts into blueprints. Crews under the supervision of construction coordinator Terry Scott could then begin the monumental task of making Zinj a physical reality.

Throughout the process of defining Zinj, Riva and the *Congo* art department sought to maintain a visual continuity between the various stage sets while supporting the movie as a whole. "The visual elements had to be seamless," Riva concluded. "The art direction had to be in the background, and it had to be extremely subtle without any elements that would distract from the story. This was Frank Marshall's movie, not mine, and the production design had to support Frank's vision and Frank's story."

Robert Woodruff, assistant art director, works on Zinj model.

October 19, 1994 / Paramount Pictures

The air is charged with electricity on the Paramount lot in Hollywood tonight. It is just past seven o'clock, and dozens of crew members and guests have

gathered around a large outdoor water tank to watch this evening's featured performer: a full-size, utterly authentic mechanical hippopotamus nick-named Petal by Stan Winston's crew. Preparations are nearly ready for the four-thousand-pound creation to charge the inflatable raft bearing several actors, including Dylan Walsh, Grant Heslov, Adewalé Akinnuoye-Agbaje, and Misty Rosas as Amy. Laura Linney, Ernie Hudson, and Tim Curry, whose characters are not featured in this shot, relax nearby, sipping steaming beverages and laughing with friends. The night is young, and they know it will most likely be hours before they are called upon to perform.

Normally covered and used as a parking lot, the fifty-by-forty-yard water tank has been dressed to look like a lagoon. Fog machines breathe an eerie kind of beauty into the night. An oar-bearing member of the special effects crew in a rubber raft fans the white mist gently into frame. A backdrop dressed with forced-perspective trees and shrubbery completes the illusion of the expan-

sive bank of a dangerous, hippo-infested river.

Two stunt hippos stand frozen along the edge of the tank. Unequipped to perform with the hydraulic and radio-controlled mobility of Petal, the stunt hippos are nonetheless authentic enough to startle the occasional passerby into a nervous double take.

A green steel pier extends a third of the way into the tank. The camera crew—positioned in the waist-deep water and dressed for the most part in black wet suits—has set up the equipment necessary to capture the hippo's charge on film. Frank Marshall, Kathleen Kennedy, and Sam Mercer watch as Allen Daviau makes final adjustments to the lighting. Stan Winston paces back and forth, holding a walkie-talkie close as he gives instructions to his team of puppeteers stationed on a raised platform opposite the pier. Cloaked in blue plastic to cut the considerable autumn chill, the puppeteers' makeshift hippo command post is packed with the computer-linked equipment that will bring Petal to life on Marshall's cue.

Safety divers are alert as the scene is ready to begin. A raft bearing a white reflector panel skims across the lagoon like an approaching pirate ship, finally satisfying Daviau's meticulous eye with the appropriate lighting adjustment. The cameras roll, and the actors in the raft, who had been languishing comfortably while they waited, are at once explorers navigating treacherous waters, ready for any turn of events—or almost any. Mounted on an underwater track, the hippo suddenly breaks the surface and charges, water spewing everywhere. Its head twists in rage, and its gaping mouth reveals a number of alarmingly realistic teeth. The actors have no trouble reacting as Petal races toward them; they jerk back with what appears to be genuine alarm. Even those standing fifty feet away jump a little. The shot ends and the crowd erupts in spontaneous applause. Winston and crew pause for a moment to enjoy their triumph, then turn to prepare for the next take.

CHAPTER•3

Information Central

The same standard of uncompromising dedication to detail that raised the lost city of Zinj was also present in developing state-of-the-art technology for the TraviCom set. With communication as an integral theme of the movie, and TraviCom representing a leading force in communications systems, it was essential to convey a particularly sophisticated on-screen reality. To help establish that reality, Frank Marshall turned to Michael Backes, who had helped generate the impressive computer graphics imagery employed for the control-room sequences in *Jurassic Park*. Marshall knew Backes' expertise would be invaluable in meeting the significant technological challenges presented by *Congo*. Without hesitation, Backes signed on as an associate producer for the film, serving as both technical consultant and liaison with Silicon Graphics Incorporated, or SGI, the computer company that would ultimately provide over $2.5 million worth of equipment to be used in conjunction with TraviCom—both on screen and off.

During the early preproduction phase, Marshall also approached computer effects veterans Casey Cannon and Van Ling, who he brought on board to serve as computer graphics supervisors for the film. Both had logged innumerable hours providing similar services for the Cyberdyne headquarters in James Cameron's *Terminator 2*, in addition to producing the special-edition laser disk for that film, and had worked with Backes in developing and executing computer graphics sequences in Cameron's earlier film, *The Abyss*.

Cannon and Ling joined preproduction efforts in July 1994 and began working with Marshall and the art department to establish the physical appearance of the TraviCom set. Once the

Sketches for the TraviCom send-and-receive video camera with satellite hookup, for use at the expedition campsites.

(top) Charles Travis (Bruce Campbell) studies the sample of flawless blue diamond eluvia during the transmission to TraviCom. (bot.) Sketch for Karen Ross's portable computer.

preliminary designs were in place, Cannon and Ling turned their attention to the back story that would provide a reality for the fictitious company. Such a back story would help to define the graphic and technical requirements for the TraviCom sequences. "TraviCom is a company that sends expeditions out into the field," explained Cannon. "They're constantly in search of new forms of minerals or stones to keep them on the cutting edge of communications technology, primarily through silicon chips, which are at the core of their satellite construction. TraviCom uses these satellites to monitor their competitors and keep on top of what has been newly discovered globally. If they learn of something that's been discovered, they can then instantly send an expedition out to find and recover some of those resources for themselves."

In designing the graphics for TraviCom, the computer team tried to generate the kind of information that a *real* high-tech communications company would employ. "We sought out information from companies that specifically design and acquire this material for government and other uses," said Cannon. "These companies specialize in capturing with their satellites data that might be used to monitor the types of projects that TraviCom would generate. Their technology is so advanced that they can program their satellites to take photographic images of any part of the globe. All of the computer graphics that were designed and played back on the set for *Congo* were based on actual designs that are used every day by real-life companies. We stayed as true to form as possible, employing only what would actually be used in the real world by a facility of this nature."

While Cannon and Ling tackled the challenge of systems research and development, Michael Backes worked with Silicon Graphics to determine the equipment necessary to achieve both the authenticity of appearance and capability of performance. "One of the first considerations we faced was deciding which computer company to deal with," Backes said. "SGI makes premier high-end workstations, and we had used them very successfully on *Jurassic Park*, both in animating the dinosaurs and as part of the computer graphics used within the context of the film. It made sense that a company like TraviCom would use this kind of equipment as well." Backes visited the Silicon

(top) Sketch and blueprint for phasic lasers. (bot.) The executed model, as used in the film.

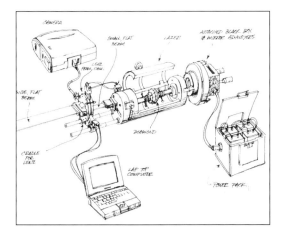

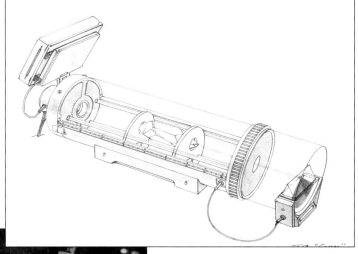

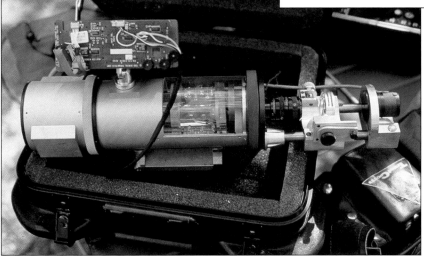

Sensor-operated machine pistols protect team at night.

Graphics facility in Northern California along with Marshall, Kennedy, and Sam Mercer. There, the filmmaking team began to devise a wish list of the kinds of technology and hardware they would like to employ in the film.

Chief among the tools available from Silicon Graphics were the state-of-the-art CPUs, or central processing units, that were the key components of the computer system. Although they were powerful representations of modern computer technology, the CPUs still had to be reconfigured to play back the high-end computer graphic images that were desired for the film. Michael Wills and Patrick Ling from Silicon Graphics worked along with the *Congo* team as exhaustive efforts were made to push the technology well beyond existing limits. "Inherently, the hardware was not built to do the things that we were trying to do with it," conceded Cannon. "Hardware of this nature is not made for feature-film use. It is made for consumer use, for people who do animation or design work. The needs of a feature film are *vastly* different, and this particular film was especially demanding in terms of what we wanted the hardware to do. For one thing, the monitors on the sets were going to receive a lot of screen time. We also had very high expectations. We wanted to do *so* much more than had ever been done before. The work was intensive, but we were excited by the challenge. We did things on this show that had never been done with SGI. In fact, I don't think they had been done before on *any* hardware."

Sophisticated, three-dimensional animations representing images from the field on TraviCom's monitors were played back internally on the CPUs through special software that was developed and programmed by the *Congo* computer graphics team. Image-processing software was used to capture the form of a gorilla's head, for example, or to reveal various other movements in the jungle. "We had some very talented graphics programmers who worked on this movie," noted Backes. "Van Ling and Casey Cannon did some programming, as did Michael Wills and Patrick Ling. Both Michael and Patrick were instrumental in rewriting the software that allowed us to play back our animations on the CPUs. They also helped write the code that created the movie files and made the displays animate correctly. It was a huge job. We had some very long animation files that we had to play back in real time in the movie. The files were so long, in fact, that they became unmanageable. As a solution, we stored the files on special video cards that used compression technology to make them smaller while still keeping the image quality."

The satellite animations themselves were images obtained

Early sketches for, and the fully executed model of, the TraviCom survey camera from the first expedition. Satellite transmissions from this camera revealed the first evidence of a malevolent presence in the jungle.

The TraviCom logo, as it appears on Karen's portable computer screen and the company's internal monitors.

from the motion passes of various Global Positioning System satellites that actually orbit the earth. Data was received from the satellites in a form that looked like zoomed photographic images; as the satellite took pictures, it started from atmospheric regions and zoomed in closer and closer to the planet, ultimately revealing the streets and buildings of Salt Lake City, Utah.

To obtain other images, the production company turned to NASA and Rutgers University for assistance. Two thermal images of the volcanic region in the Virungas had been attained during the April 1994 mission of the space shuttle *Endeavor* for Dr. Dieter Steklis of Rutgers, who was attempting to design and implement a global computer system for the purposes of spotting and tracking mountain gorillas in the remote area. The images were later used to create a database to help international efforts to study and protect the endangered primates. To these same images the *Congo* team added computer-generated volcanic smoke and ash to indicate the path of the wind, and thus—within the context of the film—enabled technicians back at TraviCom to predict where best to position their field expeditions.

As computer graphics personnel labored on the considerable imaging issues, designs for the TraviCom interior sets were completed and construction began on Stage 11 at Sony Studios. Exterior shots of the building had been captured earlier at a spanking-new Kaiser Permanente medical facility that had just been completed in Baldwin Park. The TraviCom symbol, a large, spinning gold-and-silver globe, was installed in a fountain in front of the building with the company's name boldly rising from the water. Although the hospital was as yet unopened, outpatient services and doctors' clinics were set up for the treatment of patients, and many first-time visitors were dismayed to find they had arrived at what appeared to be a communications company. A hand-painted sign assured them that they had, in fact, found Kaiser and directed them around the production in progress to the appropriate entrances.

The TraviCom interior sets built on stage were designed to reflect an almost futuristic architectural sophistication coupled with the finest computer technology available. The circular control room set was based around a central hub that widened into a formation of three rings. A domed hallway jutted from one side of the control room, while directly opposite was constructed the situation room where Karen Ross and R. B. Travis receive the urgent transmission from Charles after he discovers flawless diamonds in the Congo. Both the control and situation rooms were thoroughly equipped with state-of-the-art communications technology supplied by Silicon Graphics.

The central control room had seven computer terminals in the inner ring and seven above the center ring, along with four computer terminals along the exterior ring. Six video terminals, maintained and operated by video engineer Ian Kelly, relayed material from various TraviCom expeditions underway worldwide. Four LCD screens were featured in the center of the hub, where the TraviCom controller could theoretically monitor the other situation rooms, of which, according to the story, there were a total of five. Only one situation room was actually built as a set for the purposes of the production.

The four LCD screens provided by Silicon Graphics were actually prototypes not yet on the market at the time. At $15,000 per unit, they were unquestionably expensive, but they offered two remarkable qualities that made them assets on the

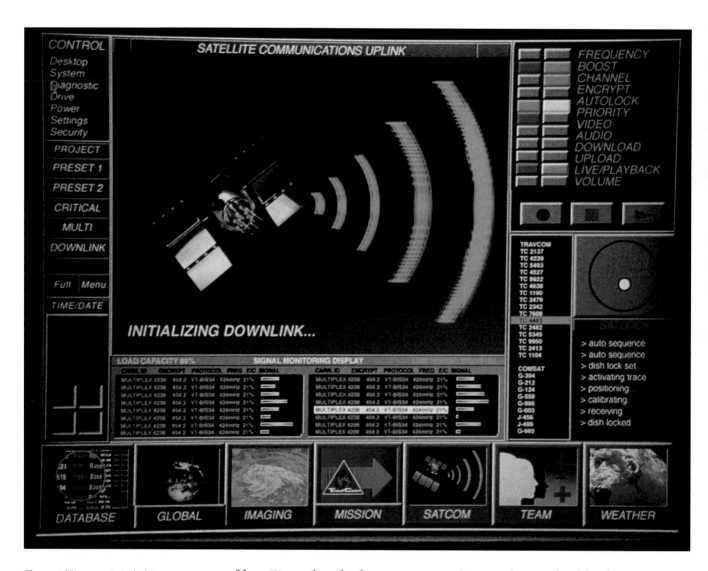

The portable computer's desktop screen.

film. First, they had an image resolution almost double the size of any other LCD screen available, and thus provided unsurpassed visual quality. A second advantage was that the back panels could be removed, giving technicians the option of slipping them off and inserting colored gels, as necessary, to support Allen Daviau's impeccable photographic style. A further advantage was their compact size. At ten inches, they were portable enough to be used as part of Karen Ross's high-tech field equipment kit during the expedition into the Congo. "The LCD screens were amazing," Cannon enthused. "Dan Evanicky and Steve Sieford from Silicon Graphics were instrumental in the physical design and engineering aspects of the LCD flat panels, and we worked extensively with them. Karen's kit was actually a prop that contained an SGI keyboard along with one of the flat panels. We fed live video or computer graphics images directly into the kit through cables that were disguised as part of the set. That way it looked as if she were receiving transmissions out in the field."

The central TraviCom set also employed four very powerful computers, called Indys, that were placed in the center of the hub to drive the LCD flat panels. In the film, a controller, played by Van Ling, is stationed there to monitor the various field operations. "One night, shortly before we started principal photography, we had a complete walk-through of the set with Frank, Kathleen, and Sam," recalled Cannon. "Van and I went over everything, especially the script we had written detailing the various TraviCom missions. By the time we had finished, they realized that the controller in this particular facility would know *all* this information. Later on, they called Van and offered him the part; and of course he said yes. He didn't have any lines, but it lent a sense of believability to have him in the scene." Ling had pulled similar duty for director James Cameron on *Terminator 2* when, as CG supervisor, he had appeared as a Cyberdyne technician. As an inside joke, Ling's old Cyberdyne jacket was thrown on the back of his chair as he monitored the control panels for TraviCom.

The back stories that played on the on-screen monitors were indicative of both TraviCom's status as a communications megapower and the computer team's dedicated ingenuity. With Frank Marshall, Cannon and Ling had determined that, in addition to the Congo expedition, TraviCom was also involved in the laying of a major transatlantic fiber-optic cable, the location of major copper deposits in the desert near the Persian Gulf, and the rescue of a field team stranded in the frozen wastelands of the Urals in Russia.

In coming up with the appropriate images to support these back stories, Cannon and Ling challenged themselves even further by vowing to use footage garnered primarily from previous Frank Marshall and Kathleen Kennedy films. "We set those parameters more for fun than anything," Cannon admitted. "We wanted to be creative and at the same time see if the trivia buffs and fans of Frank and Kathleen would notice. We spent a lot of time looking at Frank and Kathleen's past films. We were some-

The TraviCom building—better known to the residents of Baldwin Park, CA, as the Kaiser Permanente Hospital.

what limited because we needed to find footage that specifically had to do with oceanic, Arctic, desert, or jungle regions. For the Congo expedition, we were able to pull material from *Arachnophobia* and *Jurassic Park* that Frank and Kathleen had in their personal library. We looked at *Alive* for the Arctic footage and actually found some great material from documentary tapes Frank and Kathleen had shot during that production. The footage showed what seemed to be an Arctic expedition but was, in reality, the film crew on location in the snow. One of our researchers in Canada helped us with the rest of that sequence by going outside and shooting a blizzard that happened to be taking place. We shot additional footage for the oceanic and desert expeditions as well."

While genuinely functioning computers were rigged on the TraviCom set, most of the data that appeared on screen was transmitted from twenty-eight CPUs located off-stage because of the noise they generated. From their off-stage location, the CPUs were linked to the on-set hardware through a series of cables. Amplifiers were installed to avoid any signal loss, and technician Josh Kirshenbaum made sure the signal to the set maintained the appropriate twenty-four-frame-per-second synchronization required for the film.

The situation room adjacent to the control room was also thoroughly equipped. Along with monitors that displayed data pertaining to elements such as weather and seismic activity, including an accurate satellite image of the Virunga region, was a four-by-five-foot screen that served as the primary communication source whenever key transmissions were dispatched from the jungle. The unique screen was one of only two in existence, and was donated for *Congo's* use by projection specialist Joe Kane. Located off-camera was a $70,000 rear projector provided by Hughes JVC that was employed to project essential transmissions onto the screen.

For the computer graphics team, the goal of creating a TraviCom that was replete with the finest and most powerful technology had been met—and surpassed. "*Congo* was a real technical achievement because it pushed the envelope in a multitude of ways," commented Cannon. "We had some extremely dedicated participation and did things on this film that we've never done before. Even Silicon Graphics was amazed because they had never seen their hardware used so aggressively; they simply didn't know it could do what we made it do. *Congo* was a wonderful achievement for everyone involved because we realized that, to some degree, we set a new precedent for what can be accomplished with computers on film."

October 25, 1994 / Descanso Gardens

On this cold and brilliant Tuesday morning the production company has assembled at Descanso Gardens, a botanical sanctuary in the foothills east of Los Angeles, to prepare for today's shoot. The miniature biome, generated by dense foliage and encompassing shadows, has cast an enduring chill, and gaffers move briskly as they roll cases of equipment past fastidiously labeled vegetation. The elegant grounds have been transformed into the Mizumu Forest of Africa, with a sun-dappled clearing meticulously dressed by J. Michael Riva, Lisa Fischer, and crew to represent the Mizumu village where TraviCom's Bob Driscoll lies near death after an attack by a gray gorilla. The Mizumus themselves are being portrayed by over eighty extras of varying African backgrounds.

It is just past nine o'clock as extras wander toward the set wearing russet cloths around their waists and thick ropes of carved shells above.

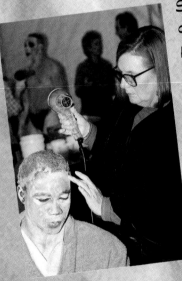

Some dance to keep warm in the early morning damp; others huddle under blankets and wait patiently nearby. Many wear terry cloth robes and slippers. All wear white makeup—meant to look like a mixture of grease and ashes—that literally covers them from head to foot. Special effects makeup artist Matthew Mungle has concocted a glycerin-based pigment for this purpose, and he and the other makeup artists have seen it generously applied. Creative makeup designer Christina Smith is stationed offstage with Mungle, in the event a touch-up is called for. Creative hair designer Judy Cory and assistant hairdresser Susan Schuler are similarly prepared to finesse the ashen locks of the players between takes.

The cameras are nearly ready to roll. A liquefied petroleum campfire is ignited, and John Hawkes, the actor portraying the doomed Driscoll, lies on his back surrounded by an army of technicians. His shoe is removed and the makeup crew hurries in to dirty his pale foot. The crowd of Mizumus—having shed their wraps—swells around him. While Frank Marshall walks Laura Linney, Dylan Walsh, and Ernie Hudson through the scene, Allen Daviau quietly directs the placement of scrims and lights, and advises script supervisor Sioux Richards to make a note of the light on Linney's hair. Smoke drifts softly on an almost imperceptible breeze.

J. Michael Riva steps through the crowd to make a final adjustment to the set. He marks the prone Hawkes with a ceremonial ocher ring and then lays feathers and foliage at strategic intervals. The background greenery is quickly hosed down to create a dripping rain forest effect, and the sound of Mizumu chanting is piped through the morning stillness. The cameras roll, and Linney and company push through the villagers to find Ross's fallen comrade. It is a good take, but countless minute adjustments are immediately initiated. Smoke is redirected, extras are shifted by mere inches, and Marshall confers with the actors as Riva slips, unnoticed, into the scene to remove the feathers from the ocher ring. He stands back to assess his work, carefully measuring color and form against the texture of the setting. The cast and crew return to their stations; they are ready for Marshall's signal to begin. This time the shot will be perfect.

Frank Marshall, director

JANUARY 12, 1995

Kennedy/Marshall had followed Congo *as a project for some time, yet you didn't initially plan to direct it. Why was that?*

It was a matter of timing. I was involved with another action-adventure that was as big as *Congo,* and I had to decide between the two. When the first project fell through at the end of preproduction, *Congo* became more of a possibility.

How familiar were you with the story at that point?

I had read the book years earlier and liked its theme of technology versus nature presented in a unique way. I read it again and realized it was something I'd definitely like to do. The story wasn't just another action-adventure: It was a thriller, it was a mystery, and it had the potential for lighter, humorous moments. *Congo* was really a blend of several different genres. I liked that you went along with the characters on a journey and saw lots of places and that the characters were well developed and interesting. I think that what ultimately makes an action movie work is when the audience cares about the people they are watching on this adventure.

With your decision to direct Congo, *what were the issues you initially addressed?*

There were a lot of technical and logistical problems that had to be solved. It was really difficult to translate a three-hundred-page book into a two-hour movie and get the essence of the story to hold up. It was a terrific story, but it was an ensemble piece, which made it even more difficult because you have to set up each character. We also had to design Amy and the grays. And then there was the matter of working out the location shooting in Costa Rica and the second-unit photography in Uganda. It was a giant logistics puzzle.

With Kathleen Kennedy and Sam Mercer you devised an eighty-three-day production schedule. What considerations led you to that schedule length?

It was a fairly normal production schedule for a movie of this size. We did *Raiders of the Lost Ark* in seventy-three days, but we didn't have gorillas to deal with. It took a lot of time to coordinate Amy and the gray gorillas and make them camera-ready. We also had several visual-effects shots and quite a few floor effects to deal with, and those took up time. It simply takes longer to film a movie that is this complex. Also, *Congo* was an ensemble picture. I learned on *Alive,* which was also an ensemble film, that it takes more time when you have to cover more people. When there are four or five people in every shot, or in every scene, it takes longer. For my next picture, I'm going to look for a little film with two people talking in a room, like the sequel to *My Dinner with Andre.*

Director Frank Marshall reviews the next scene with Ernie Hudson, Dylan Walsh, Laura Linney, and Tim Curry.

Frank Marshall explains the next shot: a scene in the geode room.

You clearly had to change plans when the decision was made not to go to Africa. As a director, how did that decision affect you?

Well, it was a compromise. I would have preferred to have shot a couple of first-unit weeks in Africa, just for the texture of it, but it would have been too expensive and logistically difficult to go. There are pluses and minuses for everything. Sometimes, when you are given limitations, you become more creative. That is what happened here. It was easy when we were going to Africa, because nobody had to think about how to create it—it was all there for us. In creating our *own* Africa, we came up with some really wonderful breakthroughs in the visuals. And we also had more shooting time because it was so much easier to shoot on the stages and local locations than it would have been to shoot in Africa. There was only one small portion of the movie that took place in an African city, anyway; for the rest of the movie we were either in the jungle or in the United States. In some ways it was a richer production because we were able to take more time with what we were doing, and we weren't restricted by the language, the customs, and the environment as we would have been in Africa. It all turned out for the best.

Amy is one of the most important characters in the film. What kind of input did you give to Stan Winston and Peter Elliott when you were working out the development of her character?

We went through each scene and developed the kinds of looks she would have. We tried to give her distinctly gorilla-like behavior, while at the same time making her very sympathetic and likable so that, hopefully, everybody would fall in love with her. What was difficult was that it took four people—one actor and three puppeteers—working together to arrive at Amy's performance. They did a fantastic job and somehow made Amy come alive in every scene. Most movies that use mechanical creatures don't feature them extensively—they use insert shots and cutaways. In *Congo*, Amy was in almost every scene *acting* with the other characters. That made it much harder.

Was it more difficult for you to direct Amy because there were so many people involved in her performance?

I just treated her like another actor, incorporating her into shots as I would any other actor. I felt that by doing that, the audience would subconsciously believe she was real. I didn't try to accommodate the special circumstances involved with her mechanics and the team of puppeteers: She was simply Amy, and when she was there on the set she was a gorilla. I remembered that Bob Zemeckis shot *Who Framed Roger Rabbit?* as if it was an ordinary film and as if the Toons were real as well. I tried to do the same thing with Amy: we proceeded as if she were a real, live character. We just put her in there and let her act and didn't cut in tight every time we wanted to tie her in to other people in the scene.

What kind of direction did you give Amy on the set?

We actually built some spontaneous behavior into her scenes, so that she wouldn't be too perfect to be believed. When you are working with animals they don't always do what you want them to do. They behave very unself-consciously. So there were things we would have Amy do that we wouldn't tell the other actors about—she'd look the wrong way or she'd be distracted by something and wouldn't

CONGO
AFRICA CREW

look the person in the eye. Or she'd be busy doing something and wouldn't come when they called her. They were the kinds of things real animals do; they get distracted very easily. In my own mind, I actually modeled Amy after my dog, Django.

Amy is absolutely convincing in the film. Did you find yourself believing in her?

Yes, and the actors did too. I would watch other people go up to her, and I could see that they wanted to pet her, but they were very cautious about it. When talking about Amy with other people, I found I couldn't refer to her as if she was anything *but* real. It was part of the magic. It was sort of like when we did *E.T.*—you had to buy into E.T. being real and not a bunch of wires. With Amy, we needed to believe she was a genuine gorilla and not someone in a suit with puppeteers off to the side. I'd often find myself staring at her, convinced she was real.

You mentioned that Amy's performance was really a collaboration between the actors—Lorene Noh and Misty Rosas—and the puppeteers who controlled the facial movements. How did that collaboration work as far as melding Amy into a single character?

It worked out great. Together they were the complete Amy. Lorene and Misty were great friends, too, so there were no egos involved as to who did the better job. I had Lorene do certain things, while Misty did other things; their mannerisms were very distinct to me. For example, there were certain ways Lorene moved her head that were a little different than when Misty did it. Misty also walked differently than Lorene. I knew which scenes each actress worked best in. It was a kind of intuition.

Whereas Amy is a lovable character in the film, the grays are indisputably the villains. What kind of preparation went into creating the grays?

We traced back a history of how the grays came to be, how they mutated, and how they became defenders of the city of Zinj. We created a complete civilization for them.

Director Frank Marshall setting up a shot during the airstrip sequence.

Their story is in the hieroglyphics that are on the walls—you can actually read how it all developed. I didn't want them to be sympathetic in any way. I didn't want anyone feeling sorry for them. Because of that, it seemed like a good idea to make them a nondescript group of bad guys. But Stan Winston had the wonderful idea of giving each of them a personality and a different kind of physical problem. As the character of Peter Elliot says in the movie, they're a genetic dead end. Stan just made sure some were more of a genetic dead end than others. That gave the performers more of a character to work with.

You characterized Congo *as an ensemble movie, and that feeling of ensemble and camaraderie was evident both in front of the camera and off-camera. Were you surprised to see the actors form such close bonds through the course of filming?*

I wasn't surprised at all, actually, because it happened on *Alive.* We had a giant ensemble on *Alive* and, amazingly enough, the guys who were supposed to be cousins in the movie became very close friends in real life. They did all their scenes together—the material was pretty intense—and then they hung out together when they weren't filming, so I guess it was only natural. The same thing happened on *Congo.* The cast spent a lot of time together because, being an ensemble picture, everybody was in almost every scene. They were a very dedicated and talented group of people and a very *nice* group of people. It was a pleasure for me to work with them, and I know they were a great support for each other. By the end of the movie, when the characters are stuck together in Zinj, they get to know each other really well. The same thing happened with the actors.

CHAPTER·4

Stage Trek

It had been a year of dauntless innovation. Preparation for *Congo* had consumed just over twelve months of some of the most intensive conceptualizing and logistical planning ever accomplished by a production, and the results were impressive. From Michael Crichton's original story, a script had been tightened into seamless cohesion; credible gorillas had been almost magically engendered; and exotic settings—established, of necessity, on native soil—had been raised on soundstages, open fields, and a half-dozen auxiliary Southern California locales. By September 26, 1994, a myriad of logistical matters had been resolved, and the day had arrived for principal photography to begin.

The site was UCLA's Rolfe Hall—where thirty years earlier Frank Marshall had attended Humanities 101—and the scene was the pivotal moment when Amy bursts into the lecture hall

(prev. pg.) The Zinj gate.
(l.) Peter Elliot introduces Amy to representatives of government and grant organizations.

as Peter Elliot is about to demonstrate the miracle of the gorilla's verbal communication with human beings. It was an especially significant moment for the cast and crew members, marking as it did the beginning of what would become their four-and-a-half-month journey together. Moreover, it was the introduction of a character who was, in essence, at the heart of the story they had gathered to tell. If Amy, a creature born of state-of-the-art animatronics, could be established as a feeling, thinking personality, they knew that all things were possible.

For producer Sam Mercer, the morning marked a significant entry on a carefully planned timeline. Beginning in November 1993 he had worked hard to determine the steps necessary to realize the production. Delineating objectives into a realistic order, with inevitable happenstance factored into the equation, Mercer had devised the timeline as a practical means of prioritizing and scheduling the multifaceted endeavor. Having previously served as a unit production manager, a location manager, vice president of motion picture production for Hollywood Pictures, and production executive for such films as *Good Morning, Vietnam; Three Fugitives; Cheetah;* and *Dead Poets Society,* Mercer was amply prepared for his fundamental role as producer of *Congo.*

Also present at Rolfe Hall was longtime Kennedy/Marshall associate Allen Daviau who would serve as director of photography. The filmmakers understood that a movie as complex as *Congo* required a cinematographer with an impeccable visual sense and a meticulous eye for detail. It was without hesitation that they turned to Daviau. The veteran DP had first joined forces with Kennedy and Marshall on the 1981 Amblin production, *E.T. the Extra-Terrestrial,* and again in 1985 on *The Color Purple.* Daviau had earned Academy Award nominations for both films and did so again for Amblin's *Empire of the Sun* in 1987. He went on to provide equally exquisite cinematography for *Avalon* and *Bugsy,* receiving Oscar nominations for his efforts. Some of his other work included *Harry and the Hendersons, Fearless, Defending Your Life,* and the American locations for *Indiana Jones and the Temple of Doom.*

Despite Daviau's vast experience, *Congo* would present the cinematographer with a series of new challenges. Among those challenges was the filming of Amy. No matter how brilliantly designed, constructed, and executed, Amy would read as a real mountain gorilla on film only through skillful cinematography. "Every creature has its own mystique," Daviau observed, "and it was my job to help create it for Amy. In the beginning, we were just trying to make *something* work. Then everybody developed a vocabulary of Amy-ness to communicate whatever it was we were after. It was something that evolved over time. The same thing happened with the lighting. We had to discover, through time, the best lighting and what angles were most appropriate for Amy; where the light should go and what tricks would make her look a certain way or evoke a specific emotion. We also had to figure out how to deal with her fur and eyes; they required some very specific techniques. These were things we discovered as we went along. A character evolves throughout the course of production, and it is a fascinating thing to observe. We found that, in reality, no amount of technical testing could prepare us for what happened once there was an actual emotional exchange

First day of shooting at UCLA's Rolfe Hall.

(l. to r.) John Dawe, puppeteer; Peter Elliott, gorilla choreographer; Stan Winston, creature designer; Bob Jackson, boomman; Larry Wallace, gaffer; and Allen Daviau, director of photography, watching Amy on a monitor.

between Amy and the actors. We learned, as time went on, to light the actors and the mood of the scene, and yet to allow for the surprises that happened once Amy interacted."

Amy's first scene, a shot of her running down the aisle at the university, was scheduled for the initial day of filming. It was one of the most difficult shots for all concerned, most particularly for the actress performing as Amy that morning, Lorene Noh. Despite the extensive research, design, and training that had gone into creating the character of Amy, there was still some nervousness and trepidation when the time actually came for the cameras to roll. "We knew, creatively, the design and the look of the suit very well by that point," Mercer recalled. "But we were still discovering the character and working out the bugs involved. Lorene, and at other times Misty Rosas, was virtually blind inside the animatronic head, so she had to be guided by Peter Elliott and rely on verbal information. That took some experience working with lines and learning, for example, how

Color sketch for Monroe's airstrip
[Johnson].

to take three steps forward and then move to the right. There were a lot of little tricks they learned as time went on; it was a process that developed quite wonderfully. Once all the elements came together, we were able to get a performance and level of believability from Amy that was extraordinary."

For this first shot Frank Marshall felt it was crucial to capture Amy's entrance scene in one continuous take. "Amy had to run down the hall and then upstairs onto a stage for a close-up, all in one take," Marshall explained. "It was extremely important that the audience see in that shot that Amy was real; we couldn't cut away from her and introduce the element of doubt. It was necessary, in that one shot, to sell her for the rest of the movie. When people saw that scene I wanted them to think, Well, that's *got* to be a real gorilla."

Acting alongside Amy were performers of the *Homo sapiens* variety who had joined the company during the final weeks of preproduction. Dylan Walsh, Laura Linney, Ernie Hudson, Grant Heslov, Joe Don Baker, and Tim Curry made up the talented ensemble that had been judiciously assembled by Marshall, Kennedy, and casting director Mike Fenton. For Marshall, the casting and development of the characters were the keys to the success of the story. "You really have to know and understand these people in order to feel scared for them," Marshall noted, "or to feel any kind of emotional response at the end of the movie. We went to great lengths to create, as much as possible, an interesting character for everybody. One of the reasons we didn't go with 'names' or big stars is that having somebody especially famous as part of the group oftentimes throws the balance out on an ensemble piece. We wanted the focus to go back and forth between Karen and Amy and Peter and Homolka and Monroe—rather than having the audience perceive one character as the lead of the movie, which is what they would have done if we'd cast a big star. Basically, I just went with really good actors."

By the second week of filming, the cast and the other members of the production team were ready to begin the tour of Southern California locations that would represent the diverse African sites called for in the script. Slated first was a visit to Norton Air Force Base in San Bernardino, where exteriors of an African airport were established. The following week took them to Hidden Creek Ranch in Simi Valley for shots of a jungle landing strip and rural road. Interior footage of the 727 taking off with an extremely distressed Amy on board were subsequently captured at Time Aviation in Sun Valley, while the abandoned Linda Vista Hospital in Boyle Heights provided both interior and exterior stages for the state hospital/detention center where the members of the expedition are held for interrogation upon their arrival in Africa. For scenes that would take place within dense jungle, and, most significantly, within the lost city of Zinj, massive sets were being constructed on stages at Sony Studios, with exterior shots set for Descanso Gardens, the UCLA Botanical Gardens, the Warner Brothers back lot, and the immense outdoor water tank at Paramount Pictures. More elaborate jungle exteriors were planned for the end of principal photography when the company would travel to Costa Rica to film near the base of the active volcano Arenal. Second-unit footage would be captured in Africa for the main title sequence and wider trekking shots.

Construction of the sets was naturally the top production priority, and while principal photography progressed on sites in and around Los Angeles, construction coordinator Terry Scott made sure they were well under way, particularly the main Zinj sets on Stage 30 and Stage 15 at Sony Studios. "I was very lucky on this film," Scott said, "because I had some of the top people in

Director Frank Marshall with Zoo Atlanta consultant Charles Horton.

(top) Stage 15: Zinj under construction. (bot.) Bill Biggerstaff painting Styrofoam to resemble stone; Styrofoam cores being made into trees.

the business working for me. We had a crew of one hundred forty during our peak construction period, and we needed every one of them. *Congo* was an incredibly huge and complicated job. I don't know how we would have done it without such a terrific crew."

Because of the massive earthquake and erupting volcano that would devastate the mythical city at movie's end, physical effects were a fundamental factor in the construction of the sets. "This was the first time we ever rigged sets of this size for special effects *and* had them stand as regular sets throughout principal photography," said Michael Lantieri who, as special effects supervisor, would ultimately be responsible for creating the

Zinj, midway through construction.

tremors that would rock Zinj. Lantieri had collaborated with Kennedy and Marshall on a number of previous projects, providing mechanical and interactive effects for *Who Framed Roger Rabbit?*, *Jurassic Park*, and *The Flintstones*, among other films. "The sets were built, for the most part, above ground like tectonic plates, so we could simulate earthquakes, with fissures forming and the ground opening up," Lantieri explained. "It took an incredible amount of planning. There were safety considerations that came into it as well. The sets had to be strong enough to stand up, yet rigged to fall in a very short turn-around time. Fortunately I had a great crew. We had between twelve and eighteen people taking care of all the effects work we were responsible for. Don Elliott, Joss Geiduschek, and Tom Pahk were especially helpful during the initial design phase. We would just put our heads together and sort it all through. We're all frustrated engineers, which came in pretty handy."

Due to the size and scope of the Zinj sets, their construction was an unusually long, four-month ordeal. "The sets were incredible in a number of ways," noted Mercer. "They had to be built all the way up to the permanent fixtures near the ceiling of the stage, and we had to figure out how to create lighting that replicated junglelike shafts of light coming through a canopy of foliage. Working with live greens added another element, and

(l.) Ziggurat building under construction; sculptor Tom Pottage.
(r.) Sculptors Adam Scutti and Jared Trepepi creating the tree root systems out of hemp and gypsolite.

(clockwise, top left) Sculptor Karl West working on a Zinj monkey; sculptor Christoph Ritterhausen creating the master mold for all the Zinj columns; special effects technician Louie Lantieri wetting down the Zinj set to enhance the jungle atmosphere; Richard Holland (l.), supervising art director, and J. Michael Riva check Zinj set construction.

our greens coordinator, Danny Ondrejko, did a fantastic job. We also had waterfalls on the sets, as well as a lot of pyrotechnic effects. The main challenge was being able to convey the magic of the place while photographically convincing the audience that Zinj was a real ancient city of impressive scope. That was hard because when working on a stage you sometimes feel that you can never get back and see it all; you worry the audience will feel it is a cheat. But the design and the way it was greened and lit, along with the fact that we installed overhead misters to create a sense of humidity, all worked to make it a believable place."

For Ondrejko, who had performed similar duties on *Jurassic*

The completed Zinj set. Sky to be added
by ILM in postproduction.

(top) One of the Zinj waterfalls.

(bot. l.) A Zinj pool.

(bot. r.) Final painting of golden pool,
outside Zinj wall [Johnson].

(top l.) Final painting of pavilion with group caught in cave-in, hidden stairs upper left [Johnson].
(top r.) Gaffer Larry Wallace.
(bot.) Early sketch of field area between gate and pavilion [Cranham].

Park, Edward Scissorhands, The Color Purple, Beetlejuice, and *Bram Stoker's Dracula,* the considerable challenge of foliating the jungles, a soundstage essential, extended to the location sites as well. "*Congo* made *Jurassic Park* look like a TV show," Ondrejko joked. "The amount of greens work was incredible. We had to cover the stages at Sony and Warner Brothers, and then add greens to the nearby locations *and* the jungle in Costa Rica.

Filming the hippo scene in the tank on the
Paramount lot.
(inset) Stan Winston examines a hippo's
eye with technician Mark Jurinko.

Every set had to be embellished so that no matter where we
were shooting we maintained continuity with identical plants. I
flew down to Costa Rica for a day, studied the vegetation, and
took some pictures for reference. We tried to match our jungles
as closely as possible to the jungles in Costa Rica and Africa."

Although the soundstages at Sony had required exhaustive
attention, other sites slated for shooting earlier in the production schedule demanded more immediate completion.
Scheduled for principal photography on October 12 was the
outdoor Warner Brothers jungle set, where a 150-foot wall of
volcanic rock—actually contrived of Styrofoam and plaster—
had been erected and dressed with greens to represent the hidden entrance to Zinj discovered early in the film by TraviCom's

Charles Travis (Bruce Campbell) and Jeffrey (Taylor Nichols). Coming across a golden pool of water, the explorers realize that by jumping in and swimming under the wall they can gain entrance to the mythical city. Their emergence on the other side of the wall was actually filmed weeks later on Stage 15, where the pool had been carefully replicated.

With only three weeks of principal photography behind it, the production was progressing remarkably well. Several more nomadic days of filming followed the Warner Brothers shoot, beginning with a trek to the vacant Linda Vista Hospital in Baldwin Park. There, scenes in which the characters are temporarily incarcerated by officials at an African detention center were completed. The following Monday was spent at Baldwin Park's new Kaiser Permanente Hospital, which had been dressed to represent the ultramodern TraviCom exteriors. On Tuesday, October 18, the cast and crew gathered at the fifty-yard outdoor tank at Paramount Pictures that had been filled with water for night shots of the river-bound safari being attacked by an

Scene 170: Peter's encounter with the silverbacks.

(top) Amy's trailer.

Peter and Amy have fun reading a storybook through 3-D glasses.

enraged hippopotamus. Construction crews spread a landing of sand and foliage on one side, and a forced-perspective backdrop was erected along the back edge to convey the illusion of distant mountains.

Working in tandem, much as they had done with the mechanical *Tyrannosaurus rex* for *Jurassic Park*, Stan Winston and Michael Lantieri devised a full-sized mechanical hippopotamus that was rigged to charge and attack the boat bearing several of the actors. Design and construction of the animatronic hippo was led by the Stan Winston Studio's Tim Nordella, while Lantieri's crew was responsible for the underwater rigging that would facilitate the hippo's forward charge.

Next on the agenda was Descanso Gardens, where sets had been dressed to represent the Mizumu village where TraviCom's

Bob Driscoll lies dying after an assault by the grays. Campsite scenes—such as one in which Peter Elliot discovers a leech on his body—were captured there as well. The company then returned to Warner Brothers' back lot for a single day to film plane wreckage and an assortment of exterior shots. The UCLA Botanical Gardens were also visited for several exteriors, including a scene in which Peter comes face-to-face with a silverback gorilla.

By November 1, the cast and crew had completed their Los Angeles area itinerary and were ready to settle down at Sony Studios. With only a few brief exceptions, they would remain at the studio for the next two and a half months. First to be shot at Sony were the interiors on Stage 11, where Amy's trailer and playroom had been built, as well as the DC-3 interior used to chronicle the flight to Africa. A week was spent filming both segments, beginning with the scenes featuring Amy's habitat. Dressed by set decorator Lisa Fischer and her crew, Amy's trailer was papered with her finger paintings of jungle images. To render the finger paintings, Fischer researched artwork produced by chimps and attempted to copy the childlike style.

By the second week in November, filming was ready to commence on the tremendous Zinj sets that had been completed on Stage 15. It would be here that the characters' arrivals and early explorations of the city would be filmed, as well as their initial encounters with the grays. Along with the entrance wall and matching golden pool, construction crews had raised the awe-inspiring, football field–sized courtyard, the Zinj gates, the ziggurats, and the pavilion entrance—all in a record-breaking six-

Early high-angle painting of mine area
[Cranham].

In the Zinj courtyard, looking toward the gates.

teen weeks. Remarkably, much of the effect of the ancient city, on both Stages 15 and 30, had been achieved with large blocks of white Styrofoam carved to form the intricate architecture. Special effects fissures and cracking sculpture were worked into the constructs, disguised to appear intact during the better part of principal photography. Placed on wooden frames, the Styrofoam blocks were roughed out with chain saws and then finessed with horse-grooming combs and modeled to a more precise shape. Plasterers then came in to complete the city's splendid veneer, and painters transformed the startling white surfaces into a look of time-ravaged decay. Ondrejko and crew followed with a lavish dressing of jungle greens placed virtually everywhere, including on the permanent fixtures affixed beneath the stage ceiling.

Using a combination of silk, plastic, and living plants, the greens department had completed the definitive illusion of equatorial Africa. "A lot of the background vegetation on the soundstages was made of silk because it would have been too difficult to maintain live plants for an extended length of time," noted Ondrejko. "Live plants would have needed to be rotated and watered constantly to keep them looking fresh. Silk products didn't require that and were also easier to duplicate. We placed live plants toward the front of the set to enhance the overall quality of the look. Vines climbing up to the sky were hung everywhere, exactly like real jungle overgrowth. In fact, we used more than half a mile of vines that were fashioned after natural jungle vegetation." Additional plants, representing those found extensively in Costa Rica, were manufactured in various sizes and placed throughout the sets as a further means of blending stage with location. Ground cover for the stages was made primarily of organic branches and clippings that had been recycled through a shredding machine and then mixed with nitro-humus and dry leaves to create a dark, rich soil that looked remarkably like rain-forest carpet. The overall result was breathtaking.

A fourth gate-head, toppled long ago, lies in front of the ziggurat building.

Relatively lightweight yet thoroughly expansive structures had been raised on the bare floors of the stages and had unconditionally captured the reality of *Congo*'s mythical city.

Lighting required an additional three weeks to rig after the completion of the sets. "The lighting for the sets was no small task," said Mercer. "There were numerous fire and safety issues that had to be dealt with. The fire department was worried about the tremendous amount of live greens and other materials that could burn. We had silks across the lights that had to be rolled in and rolled out every day, and that required manpower in terms of how we rigged the lighting. The lighting was one of the things we couldn't forecast back in November of '93 when we were first working out the logistics. Fortunately, we factored some of those surprises into the scheduling and budget so we were able to handle them as they came up."

It was through the medium of lighting that Allen Daviau was able to impart a sense of reality to the very unreal circumstances of indoor stages. "Making big pictures on indoor sets was a technique that was really honed in the old studio system," Daviau commented. "We tried to follow that example, while at the same time using newer lighting techniques and modern equipment to get the most out of our efforts. It was a great challenge, and every day we found another problem to solve, but we came up with some approaches that worked very well." Those photographic approaches included establishing a stylized look for the film. "We had to intercut real jungle exterior footage with indoor stage footage, and we did that by taking elements from the reality of both. We stylized the real day exteriors a little bit through filtration, then we took the stage settings and stylized them toward reality as much as we could. That way, when they were cut together, the two met somewhere in between. In the case of the stage interiors, we had some wonderful new tools at our disposal. One was a twenty-thousand-watt spotlight and the other was an advanced xenon spotlight that had been originally developed for rock and roll shows. By combining the two we got a light that had a quality very much like real daylight when it was used as back lighting. It looked like daylight coming through the trees, and it created a stylized sense of daylight in a jungle setting." Enhancing the illusion were wind, rain, fog, and mist provided by the special effects crew.

By Monday, December 5, the cast and crew had completed their efforts on Stage 15 and were ready to reconvene on Stage 30, only a few buildings away. The sets on this somewhat smaller but still enormous site—the grand pavilion hall, the mural room with its revealing hieroglyphics, the mine, the geode room, and the massive brick-colored catacombs—were completed during an eight-week build. It was here that scenes within the inner regions of the city would be filmed, including the climactic attack by the grays

In climactic scene 241, the Zinj gates are destroyed by an earthquake.

that coincides with the explosion of Mount Mukenko.

The extensive earthquake that fells Zinj amidst the erupting volcano was one of the last sequences to be filmed. Rigged in part from the beginning of principal photography, but not executed until well into December, the destruction of Zinj was a carefully orchestrated three-week opus that began on Stage 15 and carried over to Stage 30. "We started with shots of the ground opening," explained Michael Lantieri, "which had all been prepared months beforehand. The sets had been assembled with the kind of exploding bolts that are typically used in the aerospace industry. They were rated to hold weight while, at the same time, they were preloaded with explosives. We ran wires to the bolts and set them off electronically. We ran over two miles of wire and did an endless amount of planning and checking; but when the time came, all we had to do was blow the charges in the sequence that we wanted. Stunt doubles for the actors then fell into the cracks. In some cases we had as much as a twelve-foot drop when the ground opened up. We also had a crack that measured fifty feet long by thirty feet wide. It worked really well and I was *very* pleased. We held up the ground and had people climbing all over the sets for two months—and then in a day's time we turned around and dropped it all."

As a Southern California native, Lantieri grew up with an innate sense of the earth's propensity to rattle and shake, so the extraneous tremors that led up to the massive quake were

Protective perimeter lasers encircling the expedition's campsite.

almost second nature to him. The effect of the tremors was accomplished, in part, by using the time-honored method of building shake into the camera movement. In other cases, however, the quaking was achieved when the aboveground sets—which had been built in sections on air bearings to allow them to "float"—were shaken with pneumatic air hammers at varying speeds and levels of intensity. "We were either shaking the camera and dropping rocks and trees or opening up cracks in the ground and having steam pour out," said Lantieri. "In addition to that, the geode room on Stage 30 had an eighty-by-thirty-foot wall that was hydraulically rigged to crack and fall. On Stage 15, the pavilion set was equipped with a twelve-foot sinkhole. We also had a great big chunk of gravel—really fiberglassed Styrofoam—called the teeter-totter that was mounted on a forklift that raised it up as if it were breaking off and crashing." The forklift, which was clearly visible in some shots, was removed digitally in postproduction. "Pieces of the stage were cut loose on cue, building slowly to the climactic conclusion when the city finally tumbles. The sequence required intensive planning, to say the least."

Lantieri and crew were also responsible for rigging various laser effects. As part of TraviCom's arsenal of high-tech devices, lasers were prominently featured in the film. In the story, the characters use lasers to create perimeter fencing to ward off the grays, and near the end of the movie, Karen employs a phasic laser to blast the grays into extinction. The lasers used on set were special phase conjugation lasers developed by Martin Gundersen of USC.

By Friday, December 23, the cast and crew had completed sixty-three exhaustive days of shooting both on location and onstage. They were more than ready for a rest, and they paused for a holiday that extended through the first days of the new year. "We had spent two months on Stage 15 and two months on Stage 30," noted Sam Mercer. "Conditions were difficult at times and people got very tired. Stage 15 had all the misters going, so it was very damp. On Stage 30 it was hot and dry and dusty, like working in a coal mine, and people wore masks and goggles and endlessly brushed brick dust off their clothing. When winter came, and with it the heavy rains, that affected us too. We kept encouraging everyone to dress warmly and eat a

Lava fields on the approach to Zinj; in reality, the Warner Brothers backlot.

Scene 99: Peter rescues Karen after they've been forced to parachute from the airplane.

lot of soup. It was hard, but we had a tremendous cast and crew, and they really hung in there."

After the week-long holiday hiatus, the company returned to work to complete the teeter-totter earthquake sequence on Stage 15, followed by an immediate trip to Stage 30 for some interiors of the geode room and Zinj mine. Within the week they had moved once again—this time back to Stage 11 where Amy's trailer and the DC-3 had long since vanished and the TraviCom interiors had been erected in their place. Long days of filming took place on the circular TraviCom set as preparations for the arduous Costa Rica trip were arranged. Early scenes, most notably the critical scene in which R. B. Travis and Karen Ross receive Charles's transmissions from the Congo, were captured during the production's final days at Sony.

Although principal photography on Stage 15 had wrapped several weeks earlier, second unit continued to shoot inserts and establishing footage there as first unit progressed on Stage 30. When the cast and crew moved back to the TraviCom sets, second unit once again commanded the Zinj sets they had left behind. And while redoubled filming efforts continued at Sony, units in both Africa and Costa Rica were busy capturing exterior and aerial footage. "Running all those units simultaneously, all under Frank Marshall, allowed us to double the work," Mercer noted. "We were able to have two crews running and shooting on two stages, with the first unit going through and doing the traditional work of structuring scenes and shooting dialogue with the principals, and the second unit taking care of all the action and effects shooting. We had yet another unit shooting in Africa under the supervision of Simon Trevor—a documentarian and wildlife photographer—doing our main title and wildlife shots. A fourth unit was either prepping or shooting aerials in Costa Rica, under the direction of Mikael Salomon. In addition to all that, we had Industrial Light & Magic preparing to shoot miniatures and effects. It required an incredible amount of organization to manage it all, but it paid off. We were able to wrap principal photography on time *and* maintain a very tight post-production schedule."

On Monday, January 16, the cast and crew embarked on what would be a three-week stint in magnificent Costa Rica. Several sites had been procured within range of Arenal, the active volcano that would stand in as the story's Mount Mukenko, and filming was scheduled to begin within the week. Although the last major eruption had not occurred since 1968, at which time a flow of lava blanketed a seven-kilometer area, Arenal nonetheless spewed plumes of smoke at unpredictable intervals and emitted thunderous groans that shook the earth. By night, lava could be seen pouring down one side of the volcano, and a per-

Final painting of pavilion showing Peter and Amy unable to cross an earthquake rift [Johnson].

Final painting of the geode room
[Cranham].

petual layer of fog—generated by the considerable humidity and warmer temperatures near the opening—shrouded the top. Arenal possessed in reality all the magical qualities of Mukenko, *Congo*'s supreme antagonist.

Originally arriving in San José, the crew had, by Wednesday, moved to La Fortuna de San Carlos, near the Nicaraguan border. Because no one hotel was large enough to house the entire production team, cast and crew members were ensconced in nine separate, remotely located hotels. The remoteness of the location and the scarcity of phones necessitated the setting up of a shortwave-radio system that linked a representative from each of the nine hotels with the local La Fortuna production office, the San José production office, and key department heads.

As cast and crew settled into their respective hotels, a base camp was established at Los Lagos—an idyllic park nestled at the base of the rumbling Arenal—and trailers and equipment were laboriously trucked to the remote site. First to be shot at Los Lagos was a scene in which the expedition members head downriver in inflatable boats. As filming progressed at Los Lagos, another satellite camp was established a half mile away to prepare for the filming of the plane crash site. As there was no road into the area, filming equipment had to be carried in by the crew. To ferry in heavier film equipment, the transportation department provided two 4 x 4 Kawasaki mules. Once the site was readied, the production spent two days at the isolated location, filming the group's encounter with mountain gorillas, among other scenes.

From Los Lagos, the crew moved to Tabacón to establish a base camp from which they had planned to scale Arenal. However, when a front of bad weather set in, making the climb too precarious, Frank Marshall opted instead to film a rain montage sequence and the scene in which mountain gorillas reject Amy's advances. It wasn't until the following Wednesday that the weather cleared enough for the crew to begin its trek up the side of Arenal. Because the terrain was too treacherous even for the 4 x 4 mules, helicopters were called in to sling-load equipment up the side of the volcano.

By Friday, January 27, the production had wrapped its Arenal shoot and returned to San José. From San José, the company moved to the Soft Winds campsite, a spectacular location near the Braulio Carillo National Park. Trekking a mile up the Guapiles Highway on twisting, unpaved roads, the production established its next camp, which was still a twenty-minute hike from the location site. The company spent the next six days at this secluded setting. Subsequent stops were made at Pacuare River, Sucio River, and Volcán Irazu, an active volcano situated more than eleven thousand feet above sea level.

On Friday, February 10, the *Congo* production team flew home. Nearly impassable roads, primitive living conditions, tropical heat, exotic insects—and even an occasional coral snake—countered by the unsurpassed beauty of Costa Rica had made the filming of the adventure an adventure in itself. The irony was not lost on the production company. Like the characters who had sought the treasures of Zinj, they, too, had confronted the magnificent power of nature in their desire to achieve something extraordinary. It was an experience that was at once humbling and awe-inspiring, and it seemed an appropriate ending to the journey that had begun with such dedication so many months before.

November 15, 1994 / Sony Studios

On the set today is Jules Sylvester, the animal wrangler hired by the production to populate Zinj and its jungle environs with authentic African wildlife and vermin. Born and raised in Kenya, Sylvester has an encyclopedic knowledge of Africa's indigenous creatures. His challenge on *Congo* is to incorporate animals and

insects that would be found in an African setting into stage sets and locations in Southern California and Costa Rica.

Earlier, location shoots had required that Sylvester commandeer a variety of exotic animals: a hornbill, a bird indigenous to the African rain forest, a pair of elephants, one of which was fitted with a fabricated set of tusks to enhance its aesthetic appeal, twelve goats, a Marshall eagle, and three Capuchin monkeys which stood in for the Colobus monkeys featured in the story. Dressed in capes and tails so that they would more closely resemble their Colobus cousins, the Capuchin monkeys were assigned their own wardrobe person. Filling out the wildlife cast on location were four stationary wooden giraffes created by the *Congo* art department and six all-too-real zebras. Sylvester earned his title when one of the zebras escaped from its pen and had to be literally wrangled back into safekeeping.

Today, Sylvester is wrangling smaller but no less fascinating creatures. In a variety of plastic and glass containers he maintains the insects that will serve as a kind of organic dressing to add life and texture to the jungle sets. Never featured players, the "wooly-boogers"—as Sylvester refers to them—will be employed judiciously to elevate the authenticity and tension of specific shots. A character will rest his hand on a tree trunk, for example, oblivious to the scorpion perched nearby.

One by one, the insects from Sylvester's personal collection are paraded. There are six ten-inch-long West African millipedes commonly found swarming on buildings in the African rain forest. Naturally sluggish, the millipedes are motivated to move on cue by Sylvester, who uses blowdryers to direct a gentle current of air toward them when cameras roll. There are six-inch-long West African empress scorpions which are made docile on the set by the lowering of the stage's temperature to seventy degrees. Sylvester reassures the cast and crew that a bite from the scorpion is not fatal, but merely results in twenty-four-hour limb paralysis. There is a bright green, eight-inch-long Jackson chameleon, commonly found in gardens in Nairobi, aggressive Wolf spiders, an African bullfrog, and Madagascar cockroaches that are the size of mice. Filling out the unusual menagerie are black-and-gold tree snakes from Thailand which match a genus found in Africa, and good old American brown rats.

In a matter of weeks, the measured control of stage sets and carefully contained insects will be abandoned for the wilds of the Costa Rican jungle. There, Sylvester will contend with bullet ants, camouflaged walking stick insects, Goliath beetles, howler monkeys, and eyelash vipers that perch in trees and strike from hip to shoulder level. Although they are fascinating and wonderfully exotic, the indigenous Costa Rican creatures will be carefully excluded from the camera's eye. This story takes place in the Congo, and Jules Sylvester will ensure that only the animal inhabitants of that region will be revealed on the movie screen.

CHAPTER 05

Finding Amy

Before the Kennedy/Marshall production, all efforts to make a movie version of *Congo* had been stalled by the same seemingly insurmountable problem: finding Amy. The heart and soul of Crichton's book, Amy would also be the indisputable star of any film adaptation, and not since David O. Selznick went looking for his Scarlett had there been so much thought and effort into filling a role. A variety of schemes had been devised when the project was in previous filmmakers' hands: Amy could be played by Koko, the real-life signing gorilla who had provided the inspiration for the novel; a trained lowland gorilla could be procured from a zoo or research facility; a mountain gorilla could be illegally brought across U.S. borders and trained specifically for the film; chimpanzees could be trained and dressed in gorilla suits.

One by one, such foolhardy plans were discarded in favor of the animatronics approach that had been proved particularly effective in the creation of apes with Rick Baker's work for *Greystoke: The Legend of Tarzan* and *Gorillas in the Mist*. In both films, human actors wearing highly detailed, realistic suits performed authentically simian behaviors, while facial expression was achieved with a variety of mechanical heads. But while the animatronics work in both *Greystoke* and *Gorillas in the Mist* had been astonishingly good, those films had not presented the challenge that was inherent in filming *Congo*. The chimps in the former film and the gorillas in the latter had been featured in relatively short sequences; by contrast, Amy, who was virtually in *Congo*'s every scene, would have to hold up to the close scrutiny of the camera for nearly two hours. In addition, the character of Amy was mercurial, and a wide range of expressions and moods would have to be portrayed through the animatronic mechanisms.

A sketch of Amy wearing her backpack [Cranham].

Amy sneaks a treat in the middle of the night.

Such was the challenge facing Stan Winston when he agreed to take on the task of creating the primate characters for *Congo.* "For me," said Winston, "there was a positive and a negative about doing *Congo*—and they were both the same thing. Rick Baker had already done groundbreaking ape work in *Greystoke* and *Gorillas in the Mist;* so once the ultimate gorillas had already been created, why would we want to take the chance of jumping in and doing something we couldn't improve on? The flip side of that was that maybe we *should* do this and attempt to do it even better. I am a big fan of Rick's and have great respect for everything he has done; but to do *Congo* we had to get into the mind-set that we could take what he had done a step further. We'd already seen great gorillas, and we were in the position of having to top them."

Winston was no stranger to challenges. Entering the film industry as an aspiring young actor, he soon turned his considerable artistic abilities toward makeup effects, eventually creating—with Rick Baker—the memorable old-age makeups for Cicely Tyson in television's *The Autobiography of Miss Jane Pittman*, for which he won his second Emmy. Six more Fmmy nominations for makeup would follow, including one for Alex Haley's *Roots.* Expanding from appliance makeups to animatronic effects, Winston and his Stan Winston Studio steadily built a reputation within the film industry for impeccable artistry in the creation of ever more complex characters, including the alien queen for *Aliens,* the endoskeletal Terminator featured in both *"Terminator"* films, and a variety of animatronic dinosaurs, including a full-size T-rex for *Jurassic Park.* Winston's film experience also included several stints as second-unit director and the direction of two feature films, *A Gnome Named Gnorm* and the cult classic *Pumpkinhead.* Through the years, Winston had seen his extraordinary work rewarded with eight Academy Award nominations, and four times he had gone home with the coveted statue.

Working in close collaboration with Winston on *Congo* was primate choreographer Peter Elliott—who, by coincidence only, shared the name Crichton had chosen for his primatologist hero. Elliott had originally trained as an actor and an acrobat and had segued into ape work when he auditioned for *Greystoke* in the late seventies. While *Greystoke* would not actually make it to film for several years, Elliott was hired to conduct a research and development project for the film's opening sequence in which Tarzan is seen maturing as an adopted member of a chimpanzee community. "*Greystoke* was probably the first film to ever try to realistically portray a whole troop of chimps," Elliott noted, "so that aspect of the movie had to be looked at in a lot of detail. I went to a primate center in Oklahoma where they had set up an island populated with chimps for study. I was there for six or seven months and I

A conceptual portrait of Amy by Miles Teves for Stan Winston Studio.

actually attempted to socially integrate into the group of chimps, spending up to eight hours a day with them. Rather than just learning how to mime in a chimplike fashion for *Greystoke*, I was actually working from the inside out, treating it like an acting job—Method Chimping, I guess. It was an interesting thing to do—but I probably wouldn't have done it if I'd known as much about chimps then as I do now. Chimps are among the most dangerous animals to work with. A fully grown chimp is about ten times stronger than a man in the upper body, he has the emotional stability of a one-year-old child, and he is very self-assertive."

After two years of research and development, the *Greystoke* project was temporarily shelved, and Elliott went on to choreograph the Early Man sequences for *Quest for Fire*. Soon afterward, *Greystoke* was on again and Elliott rejoined the production to choreograph the chimp sequences. "From then on," Elliott mused, "I was known as the guy you go to if you're doing anything having to do with apes." *Gorillas in the Mist* followed, with Elliott doing another extensive study to prepare for choreographing the gorilla sequences in the film. "As it turned out, it was a good thing that I had done the chimp study first because it was far more complex. The gorilla study was quite easy, just because their social structure is so simple. Gorillas have one unquestionably dominant male in a group of females—as soon as the other males become sexually active, they are driven out. So there isn't any conflict there."

With his background and expertise, Elliott was immediately brought on to *Congo* as a key member of the production team. Elliott, along with Frank Marshall, first set out to cast performers to portray Amy and the dozen gray gorillas that would be featured in the film. In the casting process, Elliott was, in part, looking for actors who fit a certain physical profile. "The ratio of leg length to torso length was very important," Elliott said. "You can see something walking from a mile away and you will know whether or not it is a person, just because of the imprint of a biped and the length of the leg as compared to the torso. Everyone notices that gorillas have longer arms than ours; but it isn't just that their arms are long, it is also a matter of them having very short legs as compared to ours. So I was looking for people with long torsos and short legs and a lot of upper body strength.

"There was also the *quality* of the way a person moves that I

had to look out for," Elliott continued. "I could get someone with the right body requirements, but if that person moved like a rooster, I knew I would never get him to move like an ape. People have a variety of moving styles—some are stabbers, some are gliders, et cetera—and I had to consider those natural, inner physical qualities. They've been moving that way since the day they were born, and to get rid of that and retrain them is next to impossible. The same is true of people who have had extensive training for a particular skill—like dancers. I don't use dancers very often in this line of work because they have dedicated their lives to developing certain skills that I would have to spend all of my time getting rid of."

First to be brought on to the gorilla performance team was key gorilla artist John Alexander, who would assist Elliott in training the other performers. Alexander, who had toured in an acrobatic act early in his career, had—like Elliott—entered the unusual arena of film ape work with *Greystoke* and *Gorillas in*

Richard (Grant Heslov) working with Amy in her trailer when Peter arrives.

Laura Linney shares a moment with Amy between takes.

the Mist. The latter production had afforded Alexander the opportunity to gain tremendous experience and log many grueling hours of suit time as the only human performer to portray Digit, the silverback gorilla with whom researcher Dian Fossey forms a special bond in the film.

While Alexander was slated to play both a lead gray gorilla and a silverback for a brief jungle scene, Peter Elliott was initially scheduled to play the key role of Amy. Stan Winston, however, felt that for dramatic reasons, Amy should be as small as possible and should therefore be played by a petite woman. "Stan wanted to go smaller with Amy because it would make her cuter and more appealing," Elliott recalled, "and I think he was absolutely right in that decision. Frank Marshall also agreed that a woman performer might be better, since Amy was female. We went ahead and had an Amy suit made for me so that I could do some of the more strenuous action stuff, but we decided to find young women to play Amy for most of the movie."

Over the course of six weeks, Elliott conducted numerous auditions in Los Angeles and Houston—a center of gymnastics education and activity—seeing a total of nearly eight hundred people. "The auditions were like workshops. I would have people come in and walk so I could see how they moved. After that, I would show them some basic moves and tell them about an ape's short attention span and high curiosity ratio, finally letting them improvise, just to see what they could do with that information. Some people would come in going, 'Hoo-oo-oo, look how well I can imitate a gorilla'—and I would tell them to forget all of that. I was more concerned with their basic physical characteristics, and their ability to get into ape psychology."

The six-week search ended with the casting of Lorene Noh and Misty Rosas, who would share duties performing as Amy. Noh was a gymnast and drama student at California State University, Long Beach, while Rosas had ambitions to work as a stuntwoman in films. "We had originally thought that we would use Misty primarily as a stunt double," Elliott recalled, "with Lorene playing Amy for all the acting scenes. But shortly into rehearsals we realized that it was really challenging, hard work to be in that suit; so we decided we would need both of the women all the way through. It allowed us to expand what Amy could do physically because we had two different people with different strengths playing her. Lorene was very fluid and gentle and graceful; Misty was stronger in the areas that required strength and stamina."

An extensive and rigorous training program lasting eight months followed the casting. The training consisted of workouts at the Sony Studios gym, under the guidance of Dan Isaacson,

Cameraman Scott Sakamoto and puppeteer Richard Landon set up an extreme close-up insert shot with the silverback.

Dr. Paul McAuley, and Jon Moeller, to build stamina as well as specific exercises that would strengthen the performers' upper bodies—a key to executing convincing ape movement. A thorough examination of gorilla behavior was also an important part of the training. "We watched a lot of *National Geographic* specials," Noh recalled. "We also went to the zoo and watched gorillas for hours. It was a revelation because, after a while, we found that we could pick out personality traits in the different gorillas; we could figure out which gorilla was which, just by the way they behaved." Exhaustive daily rehearsals followed. "Our rehearsals consisted of a lot of acting exercises. For example, Peter explained that if a human being walked into a room and looked around, he could tell you that there was a chair, a phone, a desk, et cetera. But if a *gorilla* walked into that same room, he could tell you where there was a tiny hole in the wall, where there was a nail loose in the ceiling. Gorillas are much more curious and aware of their surroundings than human beings. Peter would encourage us to talk out loud in a kind of stream of consciousness as we explored a room. That helped a lot; when we got to shooting scenes, I found myself talking to myself in my head—and that came out in my body language."

The portrayal of Amy was a two-part challenge for Noh and Rosas: First, they had to learn the generalities of gorilla behavior and psychology; second, they had to devise a specific characterization for Amy, who not only exhibited typical gorilla behavior but also had her own distinctive personality. "I considered it to be an acting job," Noh revealed. "I saw Amy as a little princess who was kind of spoiled and used to getting her own way. So that character was on my mind, as well as the performance of the gorilla movements. By the time we started shooting, the physicality of playing a gorilla came very easily to us, because we had worked on that for so long with Peter. The gorilla part was very natural to us by then; so we could concentrate on the Amy part."

As Elliott and the performers worked to define the behavior and inner life of Amy, the artisans at Stan Winston Studio were approaching the character from the outside, designing and constructing the Amy suit and animatronic heads. Throughout the process, Winston and his team were able to take advantage of recent strides in animatronic and skin technologies—many of which they had themselves pioneered in their work for previous films. "There was no one spectacular breakthrough," Winston explained. "It was just a slow improvement as time went on. We've been doing animatronic characters for a long time, and during that time we've been developing the technology, making it blend with the art more successfully year after year. As a result, this movie *could* have been shot ten years ago—but it wouldn't have been what it is now."

The process of designing Amy had actually started nearly a year earlier, with detailed pencil sketches rendered by Stan Winston Studio artist Miles Teves. At Winston's direction, those sketches evolved until Teves arrived at a look for Amy that was appealing—if not 100 percent accurate. "We took dramatic license in the design of Amy," Winston admitted. "Amy is supposed to be a mountain gorilla, which has a very long snout and a heavy coat of fur. Lowland gorillas, on the other hand—the gorillas we are accustomed to seeing in zoos—have less fur and shorter snouts; their faces are shorter and rounder and cuter, which makes them more attractive. So, to make Amy as attractive and lovable as possible, we designed her to look more like a lowland gorilla. She had the fur and body of a mountain gorilla, but the face of a lowland gorilla. It was an artistic call that Frank and I made. We

Amy comes onstage during Peter's initial presentation.

knew there would be gorilla experts who would scream about it; but with the exception of those experts, we didn't think anyone would know the difference."

Once Amy's design had been nailed down, the Winston team began construction of the suit and animatronic head. Because of the complexities of emulating a range of facial expressions by mechanical means, ape characters have, in the past, been portrayed using a variety of animatronic heads: one head to portray anger, for example, another head for screaming, another to express a playful mood. What Winston and his team strove for in the creation of Amy was to build one head that could portray *all* of Amy's moods and expressions. "Our major challenge," Winston noted, "was to give Amy an acting and performance range that would allow her to do what she had to do as the heart of this movie. But we didn't want to have to build five or six different heads to get that range; we wanted Amy to be able to reach those performance levels with as few cheats—cutting from one head to another—as possible. With one head that could do everything, Amy could be treated as another actor on the set, not an effect."

Due to advances in the engineering of servo drives and skin technologies, Winston was able to meet the goal of creating Amy with a single head—with the exception of one shot. "We did have to go to a separate head for a shot of Amy screaming. But

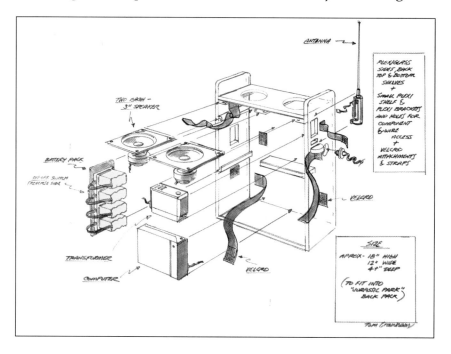

Schematic design for transmitting device.

Richard Landon, mechanical department supervisor at Stan Winston Studio, attends to Amy's servos.

other than that, Amy was Amy from start to finish, without changing heads." At one point, a chewing head—meant to be used specifically for shots of Amy eating—was also constructed; but when head puppeteer Brock Winkless proved able to make the lips of the hero head move in a chewinglike action—and actually succeeded in folding a piece of banana into the mouth—the chewing head was deemed unnecessary.

In order to construct the head, the Winston art department first took casts of Noh and Rosas. From those casts, plaster positives of the women's heads were created, over which Amy's gorilla features were sculpted in clay. Once the clay sculpture was completed, a formulated silicone was cured in molds to create the outer skin. The resulting silicone skin—which was remarkably translucent and virtually seamless—was a marked improvement over the foam latex that had been the standard material for creature work. "The silicone moved in a more organic, fluid way," Winston noted, "without that rubber look. It had a range of movement that was much better than what we could get with foam latex."

For the head, the silicone skin was applied over a fiberglass shell. Positioned inside that shell were the twenty-four servo motors required to drive Amy's facial articulation.

Mechanization of the Amy head was a task that fell to Stan Winston Studio mechanical department supervisor Richard Landon. "We built an initial head specifically for testing purposes," Landon explained. "Brock Winkless rehearsed with that head for an entire month, just beating it up and finding out what it could do and what it couldn't do, and how it would hold up after a month of heavy use. We found through that testing period that it was missing some things; so when we built the second head—the one we would use for filming—we added cheek mechanisms to make the area surrounding the eyes more expressive. I also changed the servos for the lips so that they would be stronger, which resulted in quicker, sharper lip motion." Although the test head was maintained as a backup in case of breakdowns, it was never put into service, as the hero head functioned without a single mishap throughout production.

One of the most difficult areas of the head to contend with were the eyes. Because of the far different proportions of a gorilla's head compared to a human head, the performers' real eyes could not be used. Thus, Amy's eyes—the windows to her soul—had to be built and mechanized. "We had to make sure that the eyes had the proper depth and life to them," Winston noted. "We went through a battery of tests and spent a lot of time on research and development." Heading the effort was Jon Dawe, who had made a specialty of creature eye mechanisms in

(bot. l.) Engineer Monty Shook demonstrates design progress of Amy's Virtual Reality glove to Stan Winston.
(r.) Hair fabricator Connie Grayson works on Amy's arm. Every strand of the gorilla's hair is individually "hooked" through a fine mesh screen.

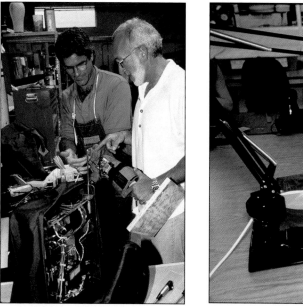

the previous decade and had developed all of the eyes for the animatronic dinosaurs in *Jurassic Park*. "One of the difficulties in designing the eyes," Dawe explained, "was fitting them within a very small space. We were trying to keep the suit as small as possible, and that meant that there was almost no space inside the remote-control head. So I had to build the eye mechanisms in an odd way. They were designed to fit around the head almost like a pair of glasses, with the servos fitting alongside the temples and on top of the head." The eyeballs themselves were cast in resin, then painted the dark orange of a real gorilla's eyes. As a final touch, the eyes were treated with an outer coating of polyester that gave them a deep, three-dimensional look.

While Amy's animatronic head was a combination of mechanisms and silicone, Amy's body was made up of a multilayered suit. Next to their own bodies, Noh and Rosas wore a one-piece garment—similar to long underwear—to absorb moisture; over that went a muscle suit that replicated the contours of a gorilla's powerful build; finally, the muscle suit was covered with a hair suit that had been constructed through a painstaking process of hand-tying and punching one strand of yak hair at a time. Supervised by Stuart Artingstall, a veteran of creature-hair work, the hair tying and punching was a labor-intensive project that required the efforts of entire teams of people working eight hours a day for several months. A natural-looking gorilla coat was achieved through an artful mixing of hair colors—reds, blacks, and browns. The underlying black silicone skin was also painted to achieve an authentic look, highlighted with subtle shades of pink and gold. A preliminary paint job, executed before the hair was punched in, was followed with a touch-up to rectify any damage suffered through the handling of the skin in the hair-punching process.

Throughout the construction of the suits, Noh and Rosas were brought into the studio to check for fit and comfort. "We went in for nine fittings," Noh recalled. "They wanted the suit to be as comfortable as possible—it weighed about thirty pounds and we were going to be in it for long periods of time. When I put the suit on for the first time, it was a claustrophobic experience—I wasn't used to having my entire body and head covered. It was also weird to have so many people working on you, touching you, checking every detail. I just wanted to crawl in a hole and say, 'Leave me alone!' But once they finished the

Scene A185: Amy encounters a chameleon.

suit it was quite comfortable—I got accustomed to it really quickly." Because Rosas was two inches shorter than Noh, a separate suit was constructed for each woman. One animatronic head, fitted with an interchangeable skull cap, served for both.

Once inside the suit and head, the performers were virtually blind, despite the fact that the head had been fitted with a fiberoptic eyepiece with a lens about the size of a pinhead that came out the corner of one of Amy's nostrils. "It was better than nothing," Landon commented, "but it was a little like looking through a peephole in a door. Perspective was way off, which made it nearly impossible for Misty and Lorene to accurately hit their marks." To surmount the problem, Noh and Rosas would work without the head during preshoot run-throughs, counting the number of steps to their marks and committing the layout of the set to memory. During filming, the women were audibly guided to their correct positions; Elliott's directions, spoken into a walkie-talkie, were picked up by the performers through a receiver inside the Amy head.

The completed hero head was powered by a battery pack located in the stomach area of the suit and operated through a set of radio controllers manipulated by a team of three puppeteers: Richard Landon, who controlled the nose flare and brow movements; Jon Dawe, who operated the eyes; and Brock Winkless, who controlled the lip articulation. With the head mounted on a stationary stand, Winkless, Landon, and Dawe worked through various expressions with Elliott and Winston during a two-week rehearsal period. "Peter Elliott would call for specific expressions," Landon recalled, "like 'play face' or 'fear' or 'anger'—and we got to a point where we could hit those expressions on a beat. We worked each of those expressions out very carefully; one servo at a time, we would maneuver the controllers and Peter would say, 'Give me a little more cheek squint' or 'Furrow the brow a bit more.' We'd do that until we had exactly what he wanted for 'fear' or 'play face' or whatever."

Following the rehearsals with the head alone, the puppeteering team spent a few days of rehearsal with Lorene Noh in the suit.

"We did two days of film tests with Allen Daviau, the director of photography, just so he could figure out how to light the suit to its best advantage," Landon recalled. "Our film tests were really valuable because what you see with your eye is often not what the camera ends up getting—you can't always tell what the camera is going to do. For example, we did what we thought was right in articulating Amy for the first film test, adding just a little bit of embellishment to her expressions, but it came off on film as being too much. So for the second day of testing we brought it way down—right down to the rather deadpan look of a real gorilla—and that turned out not to be enough expression. Then we did more video tests, which got us right into the ballpark. On a day-to-day basis, once we got to shooting, we would have to figure out how emotive she needed to be for a specific scene or shot. Peter and Stan were constantly refining the look of her expressions throughout production. Stan has a really good eye—he could come in and tell us exactly what was wrong with an expression and exactly how to make it right."

By the time filming began in September, Noh, Rosas, and the

Close-up of Amy's Virtual Reality glove on a human hand.

Amy puppeteers were well trained, well rehearsed, and ready to coordinate in creating a believable, moving performance. Such coordination did not come easily, however. Each bit of direction from Frank Marshall had to be communicated not to a single actor but to the entire Amy performance team. "To communicate to an actor you only have to ensure one person understands your directive," Marshall noted. "But with Amy, each decision, each technicality of the performance, whether minute or major, had to be understood precisely by all the people working in tandem to bring Amy to life."

After a series of rehearsals for a particular scene had been conducted without the animatronic head, the head would be donned and, working in tandem, the performer inside the suit and the puppeteers would execute a run-through, with Winston and Elliott offering performance suggestions through their ever-present walkie-talkies. "I would direct them continually throughout the scene," Elliott explained, "even as it was being filmed. Even though we had rehearsed for months and basically had all the sequences worked out beforehand, I would talk to them as they were working, just to guide them along. It was a bit like conducting music." As he was directing Noh or Rosas, Elliott—along with Winston—would also guide the puppeteers who normally worked their remote controls from a distance of ten or fifteen feet off-camera. "While I was doing sounds and speaking to the girls, I would stand right next to the puppeteers, making ape faces for them to re-create with their controls."

"What worked so beautifully in this show," Winston elaborated, "was that there was more than one set of eyes watching. This was a very intricate and complex performance. There was the gorilla performance—the believability of Amy as a gorilla rather than a person in a suit. There was the dramatic performance of that particular scene. And there was the need to watch the scene as a whole. Was the scene working dramatically, one actor to another? So there were a lot of levels to the performance, a lot of things to look for, a lot of details. There was a system of checks and balances between myself and Peter and Frank—what one of us didn't catch, the other one would. The important thing was that we were all on the same team and we all wanted Amy to look alive and organic and real."

While mechanical creatures are notorious among filmmakers

for slowing down or even stopping productions due to break-downs, the Amy head worked perfectly throughout filming. It was a remarkable feat, especially considering the complexity of the mechanisms and the amount of time the character was in front of the cameras. "This movie *should* have been the most dif-ficult we have ever done," Winston commented. "In terms of the animatronic performance, the day-in, day-out nature of it, the levels and range of that performance, this should have been the impossible show. But it went perfectly. Amy did it all, and she did it without a hitch."

In the course of production, Amy became as real to her cre-ators as she would be to audience members viewing the film. Under the direction of Frank Marshall, Peter Elliott, and Stan Winston, the singular Amy was really an alliance of performers, puppeteers, mechanisms, silicone, and fur—and something else that was indefinable. "We thought of Amy as a personality that we had to go out and find," Brock Winkless commented. "She was out there and we had to find her and bring her in. And sometimes, when it was really working, it was almost as if the controls were working themselves. Amy became a living, breath-ing thing that was separate from us, an entity unto herself."

Amy had been found.

January 12, 1995 / Sony Studios

The copper-red dirt of Stage 30's mine set is everywhere today: in the actors' hair; on shoes and clothing; floating in the air. Many crew members sport disposable hospital masks to keep the stuff from irritating their sinuses and lungs.

Dust is not the only thing in the air: There is also a palpable energy. Tomorrow is the last day of shooting before the set is struck and the company leaves for more than three weeks of location work in Costa Rica, and the second unit crew, under the direction of Stan Winston, is working at a heightened pace in order to complete shots of the grays' attack in the Zinj mine.

In preparation for an upcoming scene, padding is being strapped onto Willie Amakye who plays the unnamed lead porter. "I die today," Amakye says with a big, disarming smile, not appearing to mind; then, quoting a popular television commercial for Tombstone Pizza, "I want pepperoni on my tombstone."

Amakye has traveled an interesting path to arrive on the *Congo* set on this rainy Thursday morning. Born and raised in Ghana, he represented his

country in the 1984 Olympics in Los Angeles, running in the eight hundred and sixteen hundred meter relays. Graduating from Southeastern Louisiana University in 1985, he moved to Los Angeles the following year and promptly began working in commercials, television, and feature films in order to support himself while he continued to train. Juggling acting assignments with his training, Amakye was again on the Olympic team in 1988, but was unable to run due to an injury he sustained just one week before the team left for Seoul. A second injury thwarted his Olympic dreams in 1992.

At thirty years old, Amakye is well

aware that 1996 in Atlanta will be his last Olympics. "I had decided that I wouldn't do any features this year," Amakye said, "because they take so much time away from my training. But then last March I auditioned for *Congo* and Frank Marshall and I really clicked. Frank is a runner, too, and he has allowed me the time to train. After this movie, I'll start working on the track again, building up my speed."

For today, the only athleticism required of Amakye is a fall backward as a gray gorilla named Popeye descends on him from above. With lights and cameras appropriately set up, Amakye and David St. Pierre, the performer in the Popeye gorilla suit, are called to shoot the scene. Standing fifteen feet away are puppeteers John Rosengrant and Joe Reader, the former holding a control box to operate the gray's brows and nose, the latter wearing a remote control waldo that electronically transfers his jaw movements to the jaw of the animatronic head.

The death scene is shot several times before Winston is satisfied. On take nine there is warm, supportive applause as someone makes the announcement: "That's goodbye to Willie!"

Up to this point in the production, Amakye's running skills have yet to be utilized. "Maybe they will let me run in Costa Rica," he remarks good-naturedly as he departs Stage 30. "They told me at the beginning that I was going to be killed by a gorilla. I said, 'That's fine for the gorilla to kill me—but he has to catch me first!'"

CHAPTER•6

Grays' Anatomy

irst, they hear the wheezing, and with it comes the feeling that they are being watched by malevolent, inhuman eyes. Then they see it: a grotesque, diseased, apelike thing moving with unnatural speed, its stubby, malformed fist raised, ready to crush the skull of its victim. Isolated within Africa's vast rain forest, *Congo*'s small band of explorers survives guerrilla warfare, an emergency jump from an airplane, and the perils of the deep jungle only to face the greatest danger of all: a mutant breed of gray gorilla programmed by long-dead masters to guard the diamond mines of Zinj with unimaginable skill and savagery. The native porters call it *ibilisi*—devil; Amy calls it, simply, "bad gorilla."

Stan Winston had created such vicious and efficient terminators before, and some of them—such as the creature in *Predator* and the alien queen of *Aliens*—had suggested a natural, if unearthly, origin. But never had he been called upon to essen-

Director Frank Marshall at Stan Winston Studio during design and construction of the grays.

tially *invent* a creature that was entirely new yet genetically linked to a known species. "One of the wonderful aspects of this movie was that we had the artistic freedom to create a whole new species that had its own behavior and a culture," Winston said. "There was a lot of freedom in that. We did have to base them on some kind of reality. There were certain things about ape bone structure and muscle structure and attitude and movement that all had to be there. But we put all of that together in the way we wanted to create a new life-form."

Since they are the antagonists of the movie, it was essential that the grays appear to be cunning and intelligent enough to stage a group attack and powerful enough to kill quickly and brutally. But the dynamics of the story also demanded that they be clearly presented as a mutated, dying species. The entire creative team behind the movie had recognized the potential for misplaced sympathies from the audience if the grays appeared to be viable, and virtually innocent, animals. To make their unviability as a species clear, the design of the gray gorillas had to include a variety of deformities such as tumors, open sores, withered appendages, and bad teeth and eyes.

Miles Teves's concept drawing of a gray gorilla.

As the grays' design evolved—a process that included a series of concept sketches done by Miles Teves, Chris Swift, and Mark "Crash" McCreery, a maquette fashioned by Joey Orosco, and an early prototype head sculpted by Swift—what emerged was a creature that was part chimp and part gorilla. "We took the position that the grays were chimps on steroids," Winston stated. "Some of the facial structure and body structure is chimplike; the faces are a little longer than you would see on a gorilla; and the chest cavity and gut is smaller like a chimp's. But they aren't just

blown-up chimps—they have the size and strength of a gorilla, the aggressiveness of a chimp, and the intelligence and down-right meanness of a human being."

That chimp influence was also evident in the behavior of the grays, as choreographed by Peter Elliott. "In order to make the grays' behavior believable," Elliott said, "I had to base it in something real—and it couldn't be gorillas because they are not aggressive animals. The most realistic alternative I could come up with was a three-hundred-pound chimp. A chimpanzee will attack you, sweep you off your feet; he may join other chimps in a group attack—chimps had all the requirements for the violence that I needed for the grays."

Casting the grays during the same six-week period of work-shop auditions from which he cast Amy, Elliott found twelve performers—eight to play the foreground, "hero" grays, and four for the background animals—with a variety of backgrounds and training. The performance team—Jay Caputo, Philip Tan, Eldon Jackson, John Cameron, Garon Michael, David St. Pierre, David Anthony, Chris Antonucci, Brian Larosa, and Nameer El-Kadi—was a diverse group of stuntmen, actors, gymnasts, and martial artists. With the exception of key gorilla artist John Alexander and Elliott, who would be playing two of the most prominently featured grays, none of the actors had previous gorilla-suit experience.

"The first week of training was a shock to the group," Elliott

Early conceptual drawings of the grays (Teves).

noted. "They expected to come in and get right to the vigorous macho training; but what I did instead was make them go through a couple of weeks of acting exercises. They thought they would just get into costumes and run around a bit; but these were fully blown acting roles, and they had to be approached as such. I had them improvise and try to find a character: I let them find a human character at first, and then,

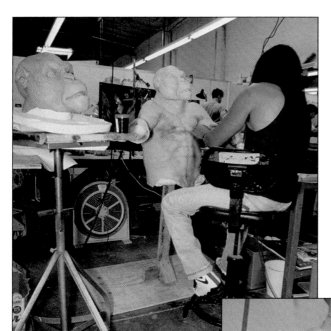

(clockwise, left) Artisan Joey Orosco builds a maquette of a gray during the design phase; prototypes of gray faces; artisan Greg Fiegel sculpting a gray's face.

Sculptor Tom McLaughlin at work on gray heads.

slowly, I took all the human qualities away from them. In the end, I don't invent the characters—I let the performers do that, and then I refine them to make sure they are within the bounds of ape behavior."

Conducted by Elliott and Alexander, training of the gray performers took place over a six-month period. In addition to acting exercises, gorilla study, and the choreography of gorilla movement and behavior, the training consisted of a rigorous physical workout at the Sony gym that would prepare the actors for the rigors of performing as quadrupeds inside thirty-pound suits. "We trained on a course three days a week," Alexander recalled. "We did circuit training to build up specific areas of the body that would be required for the ape work—weight training and jumping rope. This kind of work is very taxing physically. No matter how hard you train, there is nothing quite the same as getting into one of those suits and moving around. By the end of the training, the perfomers were as fit as they could possibly be—but they were still sore and tired after their first day in the suits."

In the course of the six-month training period, the gray performance team developed individual characters as well as a gray society and culture. "We developed a language," Elliott said, "a hierarchy structure—everything you'd find in a chimpanzee society. By the end of training, we had developed an entire social system, with communication and everything, just in case it

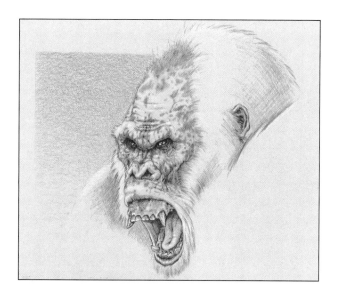

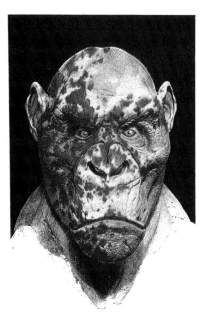

Several gray heads, as envisioned by artist Chris Swift.

would be needed for the movie. Most of it wasn't—this was an action movie, after all, not a documentary about gray gorillas—but I think all of those things we'd developed came through in the characters anyway. All of that background was there in the performances."

"The language we came up with was based on five sounds," Alexander elaborated. "Chimps use five basic sounds to communicate, so we borrowed from them—although our sounds were very different than chimp sounds. Ours were based on the wheezing, rasping sound Crichton described in his book. Even though the sound for the grays was going to be devised by the sound people and added in the sound mix in postproduction, we thought it was important to have a language that we could use on the set. It was just something we did for ourselves, to help our performances and to help us respond as a group."

What the performers had developed in the training period was not only a fully realized gorilla society but also a group of behaviors that would establish the grays as efficient killers. "We developed the grays as absolute killing machines," Alexander said. "We thought of them as three-hundred-pound pit bulls. A pit bull will keep on fighting, no matter what. So we imagined the grays as being the same; you can do what you like to these things, but they'll still come after you. Just shooting them won't stop them—you have to blow them away completely."

Concurrent with the training period, artisans at the Stan Winston Studio were realizing the physical reality of the animals, translating concept sketches into three-dimensional characters. Creative energies were at their peak as Winston let loose a team of seven sculptors—Chris Swift, Joey Orosco, Bill Basso, Dave Grasso, Paul Mejias, Greg Fiegel, and Miles Teves—to create individual grays, each with its own distinctive appearance and set of facial characteristics. "There were certain parameters Frank and I gave the sculptors to work within," Winston explained, "and certain characteristics had to be there—but within those parameters, they had the freedom to create their

(top) Finished gray heads.
(bot l.) Artisan Paul Mejias perfects a gray's face.
(bot r.) Chris Swift puts the finishing touches on a gray's face.

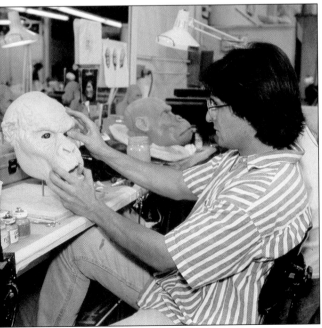

(top) Sculptor Scott Stoddard perfecting the design of the gray's hand.
(bot.) Foot and hand studies for gorilla statuary [Johnson].

own character. I think all of them loved the chance to do that." Each sculptor was also allowed to name his character—monikers that would obviously not be revealed in the course of the story but which served to identify the different grays for production purposes. In the end, the roster of grays included Buttons—a prominently featured gray played by John Alexander; Manson, played by Peter Elliott, Assassin, Bulldog, Rocco, Mordecai, Quasi, Popeye—named for his one closed, malformed eye—Taz, Critter, Moses, and Titan.

Like Amy, the grays were made up of a muscle suit to create more apelike contours on the actors' bodies, a hair suit that covered the musculature, steel and aluminum arm extensions to enable the bipedal actors to walk as quadrupeds, and an animatronic head made up of an underskull and an outer skull covered in a silicone skin. Yak hair was punched in and hand tied one strand at a time. "The gray's suit was very similar to Amy's suit," revealed Stan Winston Studio grays supervisor Chris Cowan. "It consisted of long underwear made out of a special material to absorb sweat; on top of that was the two-part muscle suit—the legs, glutes, and butt muscles as one part and the upper musculature, which went from the shoulders to the fore-

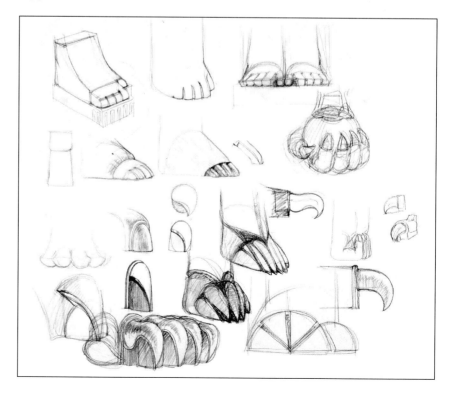

(top) Development of the underskull for one of the grays.

(bot.) Jon Dawe, director Frank Marshall, Stan Winston, and Richard Landon during a preproduction demonstration of the servo action in Amy's head.

arms and down to the crotch. Over that was the two-piece hair suit: the pants section which had the feet attached and a torso section with the arm extensions attached inside." The construction of the arm extensions was led by Rich Haugen and Al Sousa. Made of steel and aluminum, the extensions had shafted mechanisms inside that enabled the performers to bend them at the wrist to suggest some degree of articulation. Stunt versions, without the wrist articulation, were also devised.

Although mechanically complex, the construction of the grays' heads was simplified somewhat by the fact that the actors'

Actors who will bring the grays to life rehearsing with arm extensions.

own eyes would be used. "Stan knew that trying to build and puppeteer mechanical eyes for all the grays would have been a logistical nightmare," Cowan recalled. "So the heads were designed and proportioned in such a way that the real actors' eyes could be used. As a result, the grays' heads are more narrow than Amy's and the eyebrows come closer to the cheekbones; the ridge is not as pronounced." To create the illusion of gorilla-like eyes, the performers wore contact lenses. "They were twenty-two-millimeter scleral lenses, which means they covered the entire sclera of the eye—the largest I've ever seen. The contacts had almost no white to them and they were very dark. Because we were trying to suggest that these creatures were mutated and diseased, some of the lenses had a bluish tint to them. Each set of lenses was slightly different."

The animatronic heads for the eight foreground grays were equipped with fifteen to seventeen servos to drive the various functions of facial articulation. Functions included the inside and outside of the brows, nose up and down, nose flare, lip contractions up and down and in and out. Jaw articulation was con-

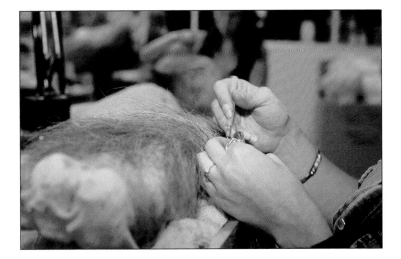

(top l., bot.) Hair fabricator Kathy Kane working on various portions of the grays. (above) Stuart Artingstall oversaw the hair fabrication department.

trolled through a waldo device worn by a puppeteer that would transfer the puppeteer's jaw movement to the jaw of the head; three or four of the heads—which had additional space for mechanics due to the structure of the performer's head—also featured a chin cup, operated by the performer himself, which could allow the performer to drive the movement of the jaw independently.

Two puppeteers were required to operate each foreground gray: one to drive the jaw and lips, and the other to drive the eyebrows, nose, and cheeks. The puppeteering teams were Chris Cowan and Chris Swift on Buttons; Joey Orosco and Mark Jurinko on Manson; Ian Stevenson and Eric Ostroff on Assassin;

The grays prepare to attack.

Paul Mejias and Al Sousa on Bulldog; Bill Basso and Karen Mason on Rocco; Greg Fiegel and Rich Haugen on Mordecai; Dave Grasso and Beth Hathaway on Quasi; and John Rosengrant and Joe Reader on Popeye. In addition to the puppeteers, each gray required a dresser responsible for getting the performer in and out of the suit and maintaining it.

The four background grays—whose construction was headed up by Paul Mejias—were mechanized far more simply and required no outside puppeteers to operate. "We called them the Chewbacca heads," Cowan said, "because they were mechanized the way Chewbacca in *Star Wars* was. There was a mechanism inside the head that opened the jaw of the character and pulled the lips back when the actor inside opened his jaw." For longer shots or other background activity, the hero grays could also be called into service, fitted with alternate stunt heads that snapped into the hair suit. "They were just foam heads, without any mechanisms. They looked really good, but they didn't do anything."

After training without suits for several months, the gray performers were gratified to finally have the outer accoutrements to visually support their performances. "When we first put all the guys in their suits," Cowan recalled, "they didn't know what to expect. But then they walked over to a mirror and all of a sudden they were really into it. It was a very exciting day for them, after all those weeks and months of training."

With the suits completed, the actors and puppeteers began rehearsing in concert, each team of three perfecting their separate duties to create one seamless gray performance. It was a collaborative process that would continue throughout production. "Once we were on the set," Alexander recalled, "we would get a lot of rehearsal time for each scene. During that rehearsal, we would go through the scene without the heads so the puppeteers could see what we were trying to portray with our own faces. Then they would pick up on that and transfer those expressions to the ape heads."

The most intense period of shooting for the grays came right after the production returned from its one week Christmas break, and throughout the month of January. Under the direction of Frank Marshall, the puppeteers and performers spent long hours on the Zinj mine set on Stage 30, staging the climactic gray attack that occurs as the expedition attempts to escape the ruined city under a barrage of spewing fire and ash from the erupting Mount Mukenko.

In creating the grays for *Congo*, Stan Winston, Peter Elliott, and their respective teams of performers, artists, and puppeteers held a mirror up to Nature and came up with an utterly convincing version of one of her most fascinating creatures gone horribly wrong. "Everybody may not love the grays as we invented them," Winston commented, "but at least nobody can say we were wrong."

Laura Linney/
Dr. Karen Ross

How did you come to be involved with Congo?

I got a call asking me to meet Frank and Kathy. There wasn't a script at the time, so I was told I should read the book. The problem was I couldn't *find* the book anywhere—I don't know if every actress in New York was buying it or what. I finally bought the book the weekend before my appointment. After I read it I thought, "Wow." Then I learned that John Shanley was writing the screenplay and that *really* piqued my interest. I'd worked with John before as a playwright, and I think very highly of him.

How did you feel about your initial meeting with Frank Marshall and Kathy Kennedy?

It was very nice, but then I didn't hear anything, and so I decided they weren't going to give me the role. *Months* later I got a call asking me to come in for a screen test. I felt pretty good about the screen test, but again, didn't hear anything for a long time. I told myself, "It's fantastic that I've gotten this far; I gave it my best shot." Then I got a call saying they were considering me but were still making up their minds and would let me know by 9:00 on a Friday. I went to see a play that night to take my mind off the whole thing. I had gone to the theater to forget about *Congo*—but this play had an entire scene with gorillas! During the intermission I called my answering machine, but there were no messages so I figured it was all over. By the time I got home there was a message saying I got the part. I was delighted, of course, and started within a week.

How did you approach the character of Karen Ross?

I decided when I started the project that I would make basic decisions about Karen, and then get on with it and go with the flow as much as I could. I went down some wrong roads at first; sometimes you try things and it just doesn't feel right so you have to change course. Everybody works differently, but for me there is usually one line that will open the door about the psychology of a character. That happened with Karen. There was one moment when I finally understood her. It was when she was on the plane with Peter Elliot and he quotes poetry to her and she immediately knows who he is quoting. To me, that moment revealed that she is a woman who is, subconsciously anyway, trying to find more poetry in her life. She is extremely bright and has worked very hard to succeed in a male-dominated industry. She has a position of authority and has to be very tough and aggressive all the time—she *has* to be. But I think she is looking for something else, that she is at a real crossroads in her life when this movie starts. Once I understood that part of her, that was a turning point for me.

You came to this production with a great deal of stage experience. What is the major difference between performing on the stage and playing a role in a movie?

One of the bigger differences is that with stage work you have time to get to know your character. In film the character evolves as the filming goes on. No matter how much preparation you do for film, until you are with the director and the other actors and you are on the set figuring out the rhythm and pace of the piece, it is difficult to flesh things out completely.

How was the experience of working with Amy?

When I looked at that face and saw those eyes looking back at me, it was as if she was a big, gorgeous puppy—I felt that same kind of pull. But Amy *wasn't* a puppy. Not at all. I had to work hard to overcome that feeling, especially at the beginning of the film, because I was not supposed to want to be near her. I needed to create a feeling of aversion to her. Off camera it was different. Every take she was in, I would go up to her and pat her nose. I don't even know if Lorene or Misty knew I did that—it was just my little ritual thing for good luck. Lorene and Misty and the puppeteers were all fantastic, and they created a wonderful character.

What was the most difficult aspect of making this movie for you?

The hardest thing was the actual physical and mental endurance required for the film. It wasn't terrible—not by any stretch of the imagination—but it was a challenge. Keeping it all together for six or seven months, remaining alert and creative when I was exhausted was very hard. The night we shot at the hippo tank, I actually fell asleep in the boat. We had been shooting all night long for several nights and I was so tired. Being in the inflatable boat was like being on a big water bed. I was awake for some of it, of course, but there were a few hours when I was in the boat with my legs flung over one side, and I was just *out*. If there are sequences in the film where you see me asleep in the boat, that's real!

If fatigue was the worst part of the Congo experience, what was the best part?

The great moments of companionship with my fellow actors. We went through an enormous adventure together and I think we will always be bonded because of it. We filmed in the freezing rain in San Bernardino and in the mud of Costa Rica—but it was great fun. I don't know if it could have been as wonderful with a different group of people. I will always be incredibly grateful for the friendships that I formed—they are what made the experience so great. And I learned so much! There were elements in this movie that were like nothing I had ever encountered before. I grew up in the world of literature, so dealing with guns and technology and communications on this level was foreign to me. It was a ball to get into that world and figure it all out.

Dylan Walsh/
Dr. Peter Elliot

When you were called in to read for the part of Peter Elliot, what were your thoughts about the project?

From the beginning, I really liked the character. You're lucky when you find the character appealing because you realize that if you get the role you're going to be involved with him for a good four or five months. Peter Elliot was very interesting to me. I didn't know anything about primatology, and I hadn't read much about evolution, but I thought, even in the first reading, that the role was something I could really get into. I was excited by the challenge and adventure of the movie, too, and I knew that when all the elements came together it would be a lot of fun.

What do you think made Peter Elliot such an interesting character?

He's good at what he does. He's very knowledgeable and has a lot of confidence in his intellectual ability. That's his forte—how much he *knows*. What he needs when this movie starts, however, is some real experience. Peter Elliot is accustomed to being in a controlled environment. He's used to being in the library or in the lab with a tame gorilla. The fact that he deals with this gorilla that's been domesticated—something wild that has been tamed and made almost human—is very telling about the character. What he needs is adventure and the chance

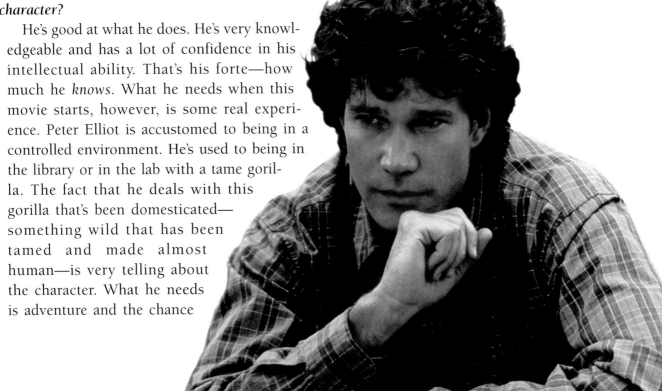

to gain some understanding in more than a cognitive way. He needs to understand things through his senses, to face some instinctual challenges.

Peter's relationship with Amy is particularly poignant, and his role as her teacher is especially significant to the story. How did you develop that relationship?

First of all, I had to develop a relationship with Lorene Noh and Misty Rosas. It was a little awkward at first, but then we had to get beyond all that and commit to the characters because we had a job to do. Respect had to develop between us, and it did. We also did a lot of improvising early on. We'd go to Stage 8 over at Sony Studios where they did all the gorilla work. They had been at it quite a while by the time I showed up; and it took some time, being inherently shy, for me to learn how to be the authority there. But in the movie I *had* to be the authority. I wasn't just some guy who was inquiring about gorillas; I was the guy who knew all about them. When everybody else in the movie first meets Amy, it's okay for them to feel totally enthralled and captivated. But I had to act as though I'd been dealing with her for years and I had to treat her very matter-of-factly. I couldn't react as if she were something strange or weird in any way.

As Amy's teacher, your character was also responsible for introducing her to sign language. Did you have any background working with sign language when you came on to this movie?

No. As soon as I got the role the filmmakers put me in touch with Bill Pugin, who had experience teaching actors sign language. We had about three or four weeks before shooting was going to start, and during that period I tried to learn as much as I could. After a while we had to focus on what was specifically needed for the film. Amy's vocabulary is necessarily limited, and I was able to learn it pretty quickly; but I felt it was important for me to go beyond that. I thought that, psychologically anyway, it was important for me to know a little more than was absolutely necessary. I thought it would help create that air of authority the character needed.

What kind of input did you get from Frank Marshall regarding your character and performance?

Frank gave direction in an easy way. He was never intimidating, and his ideas were always very intelligent and helpful. He never tried to tell me how to act—he would just make suggestions. For example, he would say, "I can see this because I'm standing a few feet away and you would eventually see it yourself, but I'm going to tell it to you now—maybe you could make a little adjustment. . . ." And he would say it with a little smile on his face, even when it was late at night and we were behind and the pressure was getting on. He made the actors feel as if we were all the same, that nobody had more to do or less, that we were all in this together. Frank was great about keeping egos in check and making sure the mood on the set was positive. He's a really nice guy—but you can't let that deceive you. He is a wonderful director, and he knows *exactly* what he's doing.

How was your experience in Costa Rica?

It is a beautiful place, and I found myself wishing that we could spend our own time there. We had an occasional Sunday afternoon free, of course, but I was so tired that I usually ended up staying by myself in a hotel room just to collect my head. I kept wanting to get out and really see the country—but then I realized I *was* seeing the country. We got to see places that we probably would never have had access to if we had just gone down there as tourists. We would take our camera equipment into a rain forest as far as we could and finally get to a place deep within. In some ways, we'd be lulled into a sense of security because the production was so huge. With one hundred twenty-five people, thirty-five vehicles, and sometimes a helicopter bringing in the food, it was easy to forget that we were in the middle of a wild place, that there were wild animals there, and that we could, theoretically, be killed. Jules Sylvester went around shaking bushes just to find snakes. Most of them were poisonous, but it was a matter of degree. Jules would say, "Well, this one would give you a really bad headache," or "If you got to the hospital in time, you might have a chance." Whenever I could, I would bring Jules along and have him duck behind the same bush I was going to be in, just to check everything out beforehand. Anytime you see a scene in the movie where I'm coming out from behind some strange bush, you can bet Jules was probably right there, too.

Congo *is an ensemble piece, and the cast really became an ensemble off camera as well. What do you think contributed to that?*

Partly it came out of fear. We collectively shared fear that we were in this *huge* movie; every day was frightening at first. We had to stick together. It also just so happened that the cast was made up of some of the greatest people I know. Grant Heslov was the comedian, and we could depend on him to make us laugh. Laura and I were both very nervous and wanted to do a good job, so we had to calm each other down. Ernie and Tim had been around the block a few times, and we were able to look to them as leaders. Filming the movie was an adventure in itself. The best part was that we were all in it together.

Tim Curry/
Herkermer Homolka

Herkermer Homolka was not in Michael Crichton's original novel, but rather is a character created expressly for the film. From your standpoint, what did the character of Homolka add to the movie?

I think that John Patrick Shanley felt the story needed somebody more exotic lurking among the rest of the expedition. I like to be exotic and lurk. I also think, for the adventure of the story, it was good to have somebody who was a little ambiguous and whose motives were perhaps a tad more venal than everybody else's. Everyone had a different motive, which made it more interesting.

What did you want to bring to the character?

One of the things that I tried to do with Homolka was *not* just have him be some kind of cardboard villain. I wanted him to be someone who tries to be funny and is, in fact, a little funny. I tried to make him a bit more Peter Lorre, at times, just to make him more interesting and accessible. He's not particularly hateful; he's a terrible old con man, really.

There appeared to be real camaraderie between the actors and crew on the set. Did you experience that as well?

Oh, yes. Miraculously, we all liked each other a great deal and that made it enormous fun to come to work. We all had different kinds of energies to play, which made it more interesting for us. This kind of movie is very much about plot, about discovering cities

and being attacked by gorillas and big set pieces of cinematic excitement. If all the actors are driving along together, it makes the story seem more real.

What did you do in the way of preparation for this role?

One thing I did was ask the producers to find a Romanian
actor to record the dialogue on tape so that I could have a
model for Homolka's dialect. I didn't want a vocal coach
because I think it is a nightmare to be haunted on the set by
someone saying, "No! It's *eech*, not *iich*!" I love dialects and
I wanted this one to be as accurate as possible. I would play
the tape once a week to remind myself of the sound. I really
made Homolka sound more Russian than Romanian
because it seemed more acceptable for huge audiences.
Other than that, I didn't do too much to prepare. I relied on
instinct, really. I come from the theater where everything is
very rehearsed and examined, and one of the things I love
about the camera is being daring about it, and hoping that
when they say "Roll" something comes to me. I obviously
came up with ideas during rehearsal, but we didn't have a
lot of time for that. I like that aspect of filmmaking, however, because I think the camera captures spontaneity; it

captures what's going on behind your eyes. It tends to see interior motives because it is really quite difficult to lie to the camera.

Amy's character was so beautifully created she seemed real. Was it easy to forget there was a person playing her?

Absolutely. It was weird. We all treated Amy like a pet. I would stroke her as if she were my dog or something. I was terribly fond of the character.

What kind of relationship does Homolka form with Amy within the context of the story?

He doesn't really care about Amy; he's not interested in her at all. He pretends to be at the beginning, just to get on the expedition, but he's really only interested in the diamonds. I had Homolka treat Amy with a kind of distanced respect.

Overall, how do you feel about the experience of making this movie?

One of the things that was fascinating about this film was that it was made by such a crack crew. It was one of the best crews I've ever worked with. Frank and Kathy were great, and so were the people who worked with them—so when I came to work, I knew I was in the best hands in Hollywood. The people who made this film were so good and so confident of their abilities that they made it seem easy and fun. There were never the kind of grim tensions that you sometimes get on a set. With *Congo*, there was a great deal of mutual respect that made coming to work terribly easy.

Ernie Hudson/ Monroe Kelly

Monroe Kelly was adapted from the Charles Munro character of the novel. Did you pull anything for your characterization from Michael Crichton's book—or did you rely completely on the script?

I suppose it was both. I really loved the character in the novel. The novel is what made me want to do the movie in the first place. In the original story, the character is the illegitimate son of an Irish settler and an Indian woman. I took the same basic scenario and made him the *adopted* son of an Irish settler. I didn't want audiences to be able to pinpoint Monroe's nationality; I wanted him to be a little mysterious. I was able to draw a lot from Charles Munro, even though, in the book, he's white. If a character is well drawn you don't get into the white and black of it. You forget all that and just get into the person. I also liked the character's

relationships with the porters and his crew in the book. Munro really respected them and treated them as if they were a part of his family.

How did your initial impressions of the character change once you got into actually shooting the movie?

Ordinarily I try to learn about the character and get a sense about him before I go in; and then once I start the movie the reality changes as I begin working with the other actors. I had a slightly different experience on this film. I really wanted to create an air of mystery about the background of my character, and I thought that having an accent was one way to do that. I went for a mid-Atlantic/British sort of accent, loosely based on Ronald Colman. That worked fine, but I began to realize that I was focusing so much on the accent that I was losing track of the person and the humanity behind that accent. You can't deal with people and relationships while thinking about the sound of your voice. After I figured that out, I found the heart of the character.

What do you feel you brought to the role of Monroe Kelly?

I have four sons and I think I'm very paternal. I found myself being that way toward Laura and Dylan. I just naturally want everything to be okay and I want to look out for people. I think Monroe is the same way. I also think he is the kind of person who will stand up when the going gets rough. When bad things start to happen on the expedition and they start losing people, it is really devastating to him because he knows that at some level he's responsible for every single person there. He is also a little cavalier and arrogant and, in the beginning, he is definitely there for the money. But I think he is much deeper than he gives himself credit for. It is only when he is put to the test that his true character comes out.

Frank Marshall observed that unless you care about the characters in a film it is meaningless when they are in jeopardy. What are your thoughts on that?

I think that's true. If you don't like the people, why go along with them on the safari? I also think that the audience cares about the characters when it is evident that they care about themselves and others. There has to be that connection between the characters. Laura and Dylan and I talked about that a lot; we knew that we needed to be able to touch each other and connect. By the end of the movie, these characters have been through a very dramatic experience together and they are bound in a way that is very deep.

Does your character make that kind of connection with Amy as well?

It wasn't necessary for her to make a connection with *me*, but I wanted the audience to know that Monroe was aware of *her*. I tried not to think of her as just another person on the safari. I kept thinking, "If this were a real gorilla, I don't think I'd get that comfortable." I knew I wouldn't feel at ease turning my back on her and ignoring her; I would be a little more attuned to where she was and what she was doing. As we went along, it got to the point where I did start thinking of her as a pet. That was right in some ways, but on the other hand there was a part of me saying, "It's a gorilla, for God's sake! She could kill you!"

What were the highs and lows of the Congo *experience for you personally?*

Costa Rica was *not* the most relaxing time I've ever had. With all of the snakes and poisonous bugs and raging rivers, there were times in Costa Rica when I thought, "God, just help me survive this. I don't want to die here." But we were blessed and nobody was hurt. It was hard work, but it was also a lot of fun and I know when I look back on the experience I'll remember it as being something really extraordinary. One of the nice things about doing *Congo* was that I knew I was working with the best people in the business. It was great to have been a part of it.

Grant Heslov/ Richard

How does your character, Richard, fit into the Congo story?

Richard is the Everyman of the movie. He gets sucked into the whole adventure against his better judgment—he doesn't really want to be there at all. He feels what most people would feel if they were thrust into a situation like this, except he voices his feelings. As a result, he's constantly nagging. He's a little negative, but he's also funny, because he's really a fish out of water. He has a special relationship with Peter and with Amy, in particular, because he spends a lot of time with her. Richard and Amy are constantly playing or grooming or hanging out together.

Because Richard has such a special relationship with Amy, did you do anything beforehand with Misty Rosas and Lorene Noh to develop that relationship?

We all worked with Bill Pugin, studying sign language together. We got along especially well; Misty and Lorene became like little sisters to Dylan and me. We'd fool around and play jokes and hang out. I think that was helpful for us as characters because we felt very free and spontaneous; it didn't feel like we were acting. Doctor Charles Horton from Zoo Atlanta also spent some time with us, and he was very helpful. Charles would say, "No, you'd never approach a gorilla like that," or "That movement might scare her." He answered a lot of questions for us about primate behavior and how we would interact with Amy.

This production was characterized by a lot of moving around—from locations throughout Southern California to studio soundstages to the rain forests of Costa Rica. How did that affect you?

It was fun, actually. It was great to go to all those different places. The only thing that was difficult was starting a scene onstage and then finishing it someplace out in the wild—with sometimes as much as three months in between. Another interesting thing about *Congo* was that we did a lot of trekking *within* the movie. We spent days where we were being filmed just walking and walking and walking. There were days when we wouldn't speak on camera at all.

What are some of your memories of the Costa Rica shoot?

It was a very intense, crazy time. I was almost bitten by a poisonous snake there. It happened when we were doing a huge shot where a helicopter flies over the characters as we all jump into a ravine. As we jumped into the ravine, I put my hand in the dirt, and some of the dirt moved away. In the middle of the shot I looked down and saw a snake moving right over my hand. Just as Frank yelled, "Cut," I jumped out of the ravine and yelled, "Snake!" But because I'm a pretty big joker, a lot of the guys didn't believe me at first. Then Jules Sylvester came down, and, somehow, he found it. It was a coral snake, which can kill you. It was a pretty profound experience.

Besides the snake, were there any other adventures that particularly stand out for you?

One of the more standout experiences was the scene where I die. That was pretty wild because it involved about four hours of prosthetic makeup application to make it look as if my head had been smashed in by the grays. I ended up looking mangled and cockeyed. I was pretty nervous about doing the scene, and I couldn't fall asleep the night before. It was probably one o'clock in the morning when I finally fell asleep, and I had a three-thirty call, so I was pretty tired that day. After they applied the makeup and I finally looked at myself in the mirror, it totally freaked me out—and it freaked everybody else out, too.

People couldn't bear to look at me. During one of the first takes I ran down some steps, but because of the makeup, I couldn't see that well and I fell. I got up and kept going and, of course, they ended up using that take. It was a very intense experience because I had never done a death scene before, and this was particularly brutal and violent. I didn't have to do any acting; I was supposed to be frightened, and I really was.

How would you characterize the experience of making Congo?

It was an amazing experience on several different levels. The movie itself was an adventure, and making it was almost as much an adventure. It was also a remarkably positive experience. I've never worked on a film where I met such a good group of people—and that's a reflection of Frank and Kathy and the people they surround themselves with.

CHAPTER 7

From the Mouth of Mukenko

Kathleen Kennedy and Frank Marshall had previously enjoyed a successful collaboration with Stan Winston; the filmmakers were no strangers to the much-lauded artistry of Industrial Light & Magic and visual effects supervisor Scott Farrar. Farrar had served in a like capacity for the Kennedy/Marshall production *Alive*, and, with the effects team at ILM, had created that film's hair-raising plane crash sequence. ILM and Farrar had also contributed effects shots to *Who Framed Roger Rabbit?* and the "Indiana Jones" films. More recently, ILM had realized the most ambitious digital effects ever recorded on film with its computer animated dinosaurs for *Jurassic Park*.

Joining the *Congo* project early in preproduction, Farrar and ILM visual effects producer Ned Gorman immediately set out to work with Marshall in determining the specific visual effects that would be required. "We spent a lot of time doing storyboards," Farrar recalled, "working out the designs of certain parts of the film with Frank. I would do rough sketches and fax them back to ILM where art director Claudia Mullaly and conceptual designer John Bell would redo my cryptic artwork and send more finished renderings back down to the production. We would storyboard whole sequences that way so Frank could look at them and decide what direction he wanted to go in."

Most of ILM's work was to be featured in the film's finale. Attempting to flee Zinj and the relentless grays, the survivors of the Project Amy expedition are thwarted in their escape by the eruption of Mount Mukenko. As the mountain's fury is spent, earthquakes rock the region, ash and smoke spew forth, and fiery lava flows down the mountain slopes, setting ablaze the surrounding jungle. While much of the climactic sequence

The magestic Volcán Arenal in Costa Rica, the volcano that serves as Mount Mukenko in the film.

The ILM storyboard sequence depicting the expedition's entry into the mines.

would be shot on Michael Lantieri's rigged, collapsible sets, visual effects would be needed to quadruple the number of grays present for the final battle and to enhance the look of the actual tremors. Additionally, ILM would provide all the lava effects for the film and would embellish live-action footage of volcanic activity with dramatic smoke and fire effects.

Although Farrar was frequently on the set to supervise the filming of background plates during principal photography, much of ILM's work could not be realized until after the location

A rainbow adds to the natural beauty of Volcán Irazu.

shoot in Costa Rica, where shots of the active Volcán Arenal were captured on film. Because the Costa Rica shoot came at the very end of the production schedule, ILM was left with an extraordinarily tight postproduction period—from mid-February to approximately the middle of May—in which to complete its seventy-five effects shots. "The most difficult aspect of this movie," Farrar commented, "was getting the shots done in time. We couldn't really begin our work until we got back from Costa Rica. That left us with only about three months to do our effects shots. It was one of the tightest post-productions we've ever dealt with."

Throughout postproduction, Frank Marshall made weekly treks to ILM's facility in San Rafael—just north of San Francisco—to approve shots as the visual effects assignment progressed. "Scott Farrar and I had to stay in close contact to work out the effects sequences," Marshall noted. "In addition to going up to ILM every week, I would review shots on videotape that Scott sent down, and we would discuss them over the phone. ILM was generating stuff every day, so the more I could go up and look at what they were doing, and the more input they could get from me, the better off we were. It saved a lot of time in the long run because it kept them from going off in inappropriate directions."

Designing and executing the lava effects was a particularly complex and intricate part of the visual effects task. From the

beginning, Marshall had aimed to infuse *Congo* with the most realistic lava ever seen in a film. To that end, Marshall and Farrar reviewed numerous films featuring lava and volcanic effects. "A couple of the movies we looked at had some very good work," Farrar recalled, "but most of the movie lava looked like pink oatmeal with steam coming out of it—which is exactly what it was." Looking for inspiration elsewhere, the effects team then turned to documentary footage of real volcanic eruptions. "From the documentary footage we discovered that a real lava flow is red and glowing, like a red electric burner on a stove. It has an internal glow, and it is self-illuminating. We also discovered that lava isn't always surrounded by fire; rather, fires erupt from the lava whenever it makes contact with plant life. We studied real lava and its effects quite thoroughly, and we decided to use that reality as our yardstick for the lava in *Congo.*"

Because of the logistical difficulties of trying to achieve the lava flows practically on the set, Marshall and Farrar determined early on to photograph the lava on miniature sets, then composite the resulting imagery into background plates shot on the full-scale sets. "Deciding to matte all the lava effects in after the fact was a tough decision to come to," Farrar admitted, "because it meant that *every* shot with lava was automatically an effects shot that couldn't be done until postproduction. But it would have taken about a hundred cement mixer trucks of the lava substance to do a pour on the set; and if we wanted to do another take, we'd have to do a massive cleanup first. It was much more controlled to do it in postproduction." To ensure that the movement of the lava flow would accurately correspond to the contours of the live-action environment, the full-scale sets were replicated exactly in miniature. By painting the miniature sets a contrasting color—in this case, blue—the effects team was able to easily extract only the image of the lava pouring through the models and composite that into the background plates.

To create a realistic lava substance, Farrar and the ILM crew experimented with a number of different materials, including varying consistencies of methyl cellulose, a thickening agent used in everything from milkshakes to building materials. Farrar and his team discovered that by adding tiny plastic beads to the methyl cellulose, the substance attained the characteristic thickness of lava. "The plastic beads had a neutral gravity to them,"

(facing pg.) Early lava tests. Special effects technician Steve Bunyea worked with a number of materials during these tests. (this pg.) ILM at work on the lava sequences: (top) Model shop project supervisor Lorne Peterson. (bot.) Model makers Bob Cooper (l.) and Brian Gernand (r.).

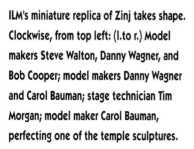

ILM's miniature replica of Zinj takes shape. Clockwise, from top left: (l.to r.) Model makers Steve Walton, Danny Wagner, and Bob Cooper; model makers Danny Wagner and Carol Bauman; stage technician Tim Morgan; model maker Carol Bauman, perfecting one of the temple sculptures.

Farrar noted, "which meant they didn't float to the top of the liquid or sink to the bottom. They stayed wherever we put them, and if we put in enough of them, they maintained the bulk of the liquid."

To create the sooty crust which forms on real lava, the effects team sprinkled black and gray tempura pigments on top of the methyl cellulose, which, while naturally clear, was also mixed with white tempura, in part to ensure easy matte extraction when the lava mixture was photographed against miniature sets that had been painted blue. Starting with a white liquid also gave the effects team more control in determining its ultimate coloration. "We thought that it would be better to photograph the lava white, and then add the red color after the fact," said Farrar. "By starting with a white substance, scanning that into the computer, then adding color to it with a computer paint program, we were able to get all kinds of variations from yellow to orange to red. It also created the illusion that the material was internally lit, just as real lava is. By the time we were done with it, it was by far the best-looking man-made lava we'd ever seen. It was red and bubbling and very realistic."

Farrar and his ILM crew also had to simulate the interaction of the lava and the surrounding foliage. Foliage in the path of the lava flow on the real sets was removed for the filming of the background plates. Then, to create the combustive meeting of the lava with vegetation, burning foliage was shot as a separate element and added to the final composite. A variety of smoke effects also had to be devised to support the look of an erupting volcano and vapors coming off the smoldering lava and burning landscape. Again, the effects team relied on footage of real volcanic eruptions for reference. "If you look at images of Mount

(bottom l.) Model maker Geoff Lake (l.), stage technician Tim Morgan and model maker J.D. Durst refine the miniature jungle set outside the Zinj temple. (top r.) Chief model maker Mike Lynch.
(bottom r.) Model maker Steve Walton.

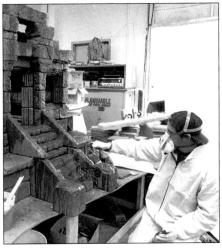

At ILM, the volcanic eruption and resultant lava flow are set up using a blue screen process that will later be combined with the live-action shot. (l.) Model makers Robbie Edwards and Scott McNamera, chief model makers Eben Stromquist and Mike Lynch, and stage technician Berny Demolski. (r.) Effects cameraman John Fante.

St. Helens erupting," said Farrar, "you see that it is sort of curly, tufted, heavy smoke. It isn't the kind of wispy smoke you get when you light a campfire. To get some of our smoke elements, we photographed real smoke, going out to an isolated area and starting huge fires. Then we matted those smoke elements into the plates we shot in Costa Rica." Combined with the real-world footage were layers of computer-generated smoke elements. CG was also instrumental in creating the illusion of distant fires for wide shots of the jungle engulfed in flames. "There were some shots that required dozens of fires all over the mountain. We found that it was easier to simulate those background fires with computer-generated elements, rather than shooting a lot of fire on stage and having to matte it in. The CG was only useful for the distant fires, however, where you could only discern a vague glow. For really good-looking foreground fire, we still had to shoot a practical element and matte it into the plate."

ILM's work was evident not only in shots revealing Mukenko's fury but also in the mines where the survivors of the Project Amy expedition stage their final battle against the grays as the city collapses around them. Within the mines, the group is surrounded by what appears to be dozens of grays. Since only twelve grays had been provided, it was up to ILM to increase their number through visual effects. To achieve the multiplied effect, a group of grays was shot in one area of the mine set. The group was then moved to another position on the set and filmed again. This process was repeated numerous times, and the resulting shots were combined, creating the illusion of forty to sixty advancing, menacing grays.

Because the combined elements would require grays to pass in front and behind each other, the effects effort for the mine battle sequence involved extensive rotoscoping. Prior to the development of digital tools, rotoscoping was a painstaking process by which an artist would trace a projected image onto a piece of paper, thus creating mattes that would enable separately filmed elements to blend and interact appropriately in the final composite. Though still an exacting skill, the rotoscoping for *Congo* was done entirely on the computer, which streamlined the process considerably. "We had to do a lot of digital rotoscoping for shots of the grays in the mines," ILM digital matte artist Paul

As Zinj is destroyed by an earthquake and the eruption of Mount Mukenko, the members of the expedition flee for their lives.

Huston said. "For example, we would have one group of grays positioned high up in the set, scrambling around and jumping down onto the lower levels, crossing in front of grays that had been shot separately on the lower level. So the grays that were falling from the higher level had to be matted across the grays that were on the lower level. The rotoscoping for all of that was done on the computer. It would have been nearly impossible to do such complicated rotoscope mattes traditionally."

As the members of the *Congo* expedition make their escape from the collapsing ruins of Zinj, the grays are overtaken by the lava. The ultimate annihilation of the degenerate species is clearly demonstrated in a series of dramatic shots of the grays' fiery disintegration upon contact with the molten rock. "One thing that Frank stressed," Farrar said, "was that he wanted it to be absolutely clear that the grays are wiped out by the end of the movie. So at one point lava comes flowing out of the geode room after the mountain erupts and the whole mine area becomes submerged in a pool of lava. Any of the grays that are left at that point fall into this lava and are disintegrated." To achieve the sequence, gray performers were first shot falling

The ILM storyboard depicting Peter's harrowing escape from the fiery lava flow—and the actual frame blowup of the finished composite shot of the same scene.

The final ILM composite shots showing Peter and Amy trying to outrun the onrushing lava as it flows through the ruins of Zinj.

from the sides of the mine walls onto stunt pads. The stunt pads were then removed for filming of the visual effects background plates. "We added a tiny splash and ash element as an aftereffect. Because the grays flame up and vaporize as soon as they hit the lava, there wasn't much need to show the interaction between the animals and the lava. For the most part, we were able to realize the vaporizing of the grays by setting little gray forms on fire. These forms were made out of pyrotechnic elements and steel wool that we could ignite and burn. We would photograph these forms igniting, then position the resulting elements into the plates of the grays jumping from the mine walls. We also had some full-size gray dummies that we were able to set on fire. In general, we accomplished the sequence by showing a succession of all these different versions of grays—the real performers, the dummies, and the miniature forms—quickly dissolving one into another."

Other shots in the climactic battle sequence revealed grays being destroyed by the high-tech phasic laser wielded by Karen Ross. Although authentic laser equipment had been used during live-action photography, most of the film's laser beam effects—particularly those featuring the beam's interaction with the grays—were provided by ILM. "There was a shot of a gray being burned through by the laser," Farrar said, "and another shot where a gray gets his arm blown off by the laser blast. For all those shots, we created computer-animated laser beams that were composited into the live-action plates."

With the grays destroyed, the survivors finally make their way out of the jungle in a hot air balloon. The airborne escape sequence included dialogue scenes shot in Simi Valley with both the camera and the gondola carrying the actors hung high on hundred-foot crane arms. "Both the camera and the gondola were moving through the air on these cranes," Farrar explained. "It was a really good way to get those shots, because it provided a natural sky background." Such a practical approach would not suffice, however, for subsequent panoramic aerial shots of the balloon drifting by Mukenko's burning slopes. To capture the spectacular view on film, an aerial plate of the balloon and Volcán

(facing pg.) The final ILM composite—Karen Ross peers up at the astonishing diamond deposit inside the geode room. (bot.) Abandoned equipment and a sulphurous pool outside the entrance to the mines. (below) Eyes on the prize: Homolka grasps one of the priceless Zinj diamonds.

Peter and Karen escape the destruction in a hot-air balloon.

Arenal in the background was shot from a helicopter. "The production shot a beautiful plate in Costa Rica of the balloon passing by the sun and the mountain during a sunrise—which worked as a sunset for the purposes of the story. What we had to add to that was the background of Mukenko with the lava flowing down and the smoke coming out the top. To do that, we constructed a miniature section of the mountain that we photographed to represent all the major destruction and volcanic activity our characters see from the point of view of their balloon. We basically created a 'cap' that had rivulets of lava running down its sides. That miniature photography was matted back into the footage of Volcán Arenal. It was an almost entirely fabricated shot, but it looked great and it provided a big, dramatic finish to the story."

While the majority of ILM's work was featured in the final act of the movie, a smattering of other visual effects appear throughout the film. ILM was responsible for the missiles fired at the expedition's chartered plane by ground troops early in the story. "We shot plates that revealed the guerrillas firing weapons toward a plane flying by," explained Farrar, "but there were obviously no missiles in those shots. So we put in the missiles, as well as the rocket trails they left behind and, in certain shots, resulting explosions. The missiles themselves were all computer generated. It was quicker and gave us more flexibility to create the missiles in CG rather than building physical models. We also did a shot of a final missile hitting the plane and blowing it up after our characters have parachuted out."

Less explosive but equally vital were effects which helped to support the visual design of the film. Such effects included the replacement of the lighting grid that ran across the ceiling of Stage 15 with a realistic jungle canopy. To realize the canopy, Farrar sent Paul Huston to a location in Guatemala to shoot a number of still photos. Those photos of jungle flora were matted into the plates shot on stage, then digitally manipulated to make the still-photographed foliage move in a realistic fashion. In

The eruption of Mount Mukenko at ILM, orchestrated by stage technicians Gus Pollek and Berny Demolski.

some cases, foreground foliage was shot as a separate element and positioned in front of the still photography.

Similarly, ILM was called upon to extend the expansive mine set in order to create an even more dramatically compelling setting for the climax of the film. "Frank wanted to make the walls

of the mine look higher," Farrar noted. "To do that, we took sections of the walls and replicated them in the computer, adding those sections to the top of the filmed set to create a higher and bigger room. It was a beautiful set, so all we did was enhance the size and complete the top section. Frank also wanted the geode room that was in the back of the mine to look as if it was even *farther* back than it was onstage. So we had to make the entire mine set look much longer, adding sections like a patchwork puzzle." The geode room set itself was also finished off through visual effects. One scene in particular, in which the expedition first discovers the enormous geological heart of diamond within the mines, required the creation of an incredible, diamond-studded ceiling. "The actual geode room set just had lights up there—there was nothing in the ceiling at all. So we created this tube of jewels for the ceiling in postproduction. It was an exquisite looking miniature made of aluminum foil painted black. It was about ten feet long, with little holes in it which enabled us to light it from behind to create the jeweled effect. We dressed it with crystals—some of which were several hundred dollars apiece. Those were placed in the model and lit from behind by hidden light sources. We also took crystals and put them on a tabletop and separately lit them and photographed them in many different intricate ways to get a series of twinkle effects on film. All of those separate elements were combined and matted into the ceiling area of the geode room."

It was the creation of just such subtle yet production-enhancing effects that made the efforts of Scott Farrar and the artisans at Industrial Light & Magic an integral part of the making of *Congo*. It was a role they had filled many, many times—and yet there was, as always, a sense of discovery and invention as they completed their *Congo* assignment. "It seems that effects are always prototypical," Farrar commented. "Even though people shoot movies every day, any given shot in one way or another is not the same as any other shot. There is always something new that you have to deal with. There is always something to figure out. That is just the nature of a big film like *Congo*."

(facing pg.) The piles of bones outside the entrance to the mines, grisly evidence of the fate of past explorers. (bot.) Peter, Karen, Monroe, and company approach the entrance to the geode room.

January 21, 1995

Los Lagos, Costa Rica

This Saturday morning the company is far removed from the paper-reading, coffee-sipping comfort of an ordinary Hollywood weekend. It is the production's fifth day on location in Costa Rica, and there isn't a cushioned sofa or *Los Angeles Times* in sight. Instead, the cast and crew have gathered near the base of Volcán Arenal where they are preparing to shoot an interaction between Amy and three mountain gorillas against the spectacular backdrop of a living, boulder-spewing volcano.

Under the stalwart direction of Frank Marshall, the company is beginning its second day at this magnificent and isolated site—a satellite camp that has been established a half-mile's hike from the main base camp at Los Lagos. Days earlier, Arenal had remained veiled in cloud cover and, with the exception of a single impressive explosion, the *Congo* troupe easily forgot they were within a few miles of a potentially overpowering force of nature. Not so on Friday. The sky shone brilliantly clear throughout the day, and Arenal performed without reserve. Mushroom clouds of gas and steam billowed from the crater, while rocks and boulders were launched from someplace deep within the earth and tumbled down the mountainside, kicking up avalanches of volcanic dust en route.

With Friday's seismic performance in mind, Marshall is hopeful as the crew prepares for this morning's shoot. Arenal rises prominently in the background, and camera equipment is raised and adjusted to capture the full glory of the image. Lorene Noh, as Amy, is suited up for the slated scene and relaxes on the grassy slopes nearby. Key gorilla artist John Alexander stands ready to perform as a silverback alongside Peter

Elliott and David Anthony, outfitted as blackback gorillas. The moment is underscored by the haunting bay of howler monkeys in the distance, a moving reminder of both the sacred and feral nature of their surroundings.

The cameras are nearly set to roll for the first shot of the day when, suddenly, Arenal bursts forth with an extraordinary explosion mere moments before filming begins. For the remainder of the morning, Marshall watches and waits, looking expectantly toward Arenal in hopes of capturing a repeat performance on film. But Arenal remains calm, supremely indifferent to the schedules and needs of the production company camped out on her slopes. Finally, the crew breaks for lunch. With the cameras idle, Marshall can only watch helplessly as Arenal again explodes in spectacular fashion. Quickly navigating the trail back to the satellite camp, the director arrives to the good news that the ILM camera was set up and rolling. The event has been photographed and will be easily intercut with the gorilla scene later in the production schedule.

The afternoon brings an off-camera danger completely unrelated to volcanic splendor: a deadly pit viper is discovered comfortably curled in the grass beneath the chair of hairstylist Judy Cory. Alarm radiates throughout the crew, but Jules Sylvester, with characteristic enthusiasm and skill, deftly snares the creature with his snake stick and displays it proudly. The viper is cautiously admired and then released, unharmed, within more comfortable proximity. Nervous laughter is followed by a thoughtful quiet as the company returns to the task at hand. They have only a few hours of daylight left before wrapping at this site, and the sky is growing increasingly more threatening.

CHAPTER • 8

Postscript

By the end of February 1995, four and a half months of shooting had been completed; the actors, department heads, and crew members had gone on to other projects; the animatronic accoutrements which had made up Amy and the grays had been carefully put into storage at the Stan Winston Studio. But for Frank Marshall the process of making *Congo* was far from over. Many crucial tasks still had to be attended to before the film's June 9 release, and the exhausting pace of the production schedule did not let up as Marshall continued to finalize the film throughout the twelve-week postproduction.

In addition to overseeing the ongoing visual effects work that was being diligently pursued at Industrial Light & Magic, Marshall concerned himself during this period with realizing a final cut of the film with Anne V. Coates, a venerated editor who had been nominated for Academy Awards four times throughout her long career. Coates had won the Oscar for her work on David Lean's classic *Lawrence of Arabia*; subsequent nods from the Academy had been earned for *Becket, The Elephant Man,* and *In the Line of Fire.* Although Coates had been on the *Congo* production since a week before filming began, her most intense period of collaboration with Marshall did not begin until the shooting had come to a close. "While we were still shooting," Marshall recalled, "I would only see Anne at lunch. During that time, we'd talk about specific scenes. She would make suggestions such as, 'We could use another close-up,' or 'It would be nice if we had another shot of this character.' I needed her input while I was still shooting on that particular set, because it allowed me to go back and get those shots. After our lunch meetings, Anne would go back to the cutting room and con-

Academy-award winning film editor
Anne V. Coates, working on the Lightworks
electronic editing system.

struct scenes based on the ideas we had discussed."

As it had for nearly everyone involved, *Congo* would present Coates with an entirely new challenge. After more than forty years of editing movies through tried-and-true techniques—which essentially consisted of viewing actual film frames on a movieola and physically making the appropriate cuts—Coates would cut *Congo* on three Lightworks electronic editing systems. Although similar equipment had commonly been used in television video productions for years, the electronic approach was still relatively new to the feature film arena at the time *Congo* was being completed. "It had always seemed to me that we had all this great technology out there, but that we were reluctant to apply it to the movie business," Marshall commented. "That has been especially true in editing. For nearly a hundred years, ever since movies were first made, editing has been done pretty much with scissors and a piece of tape. Film editors have been reluctant to take advantage of electronic editing; but with the computer power we have now, it is here to stay. For *Congo*, I thought the time had come to make the leap."

Making the transition from handling actual film to dealing with images made up of nothing more than computer pixels proved to be somewhat of an adjustment for Coates. "It took me some time to get accustomed to it," Coates admitted. "I have always loved film, and I was happy working with film, so I didn't take like a duck to water to the Lightworks. Normally, I would actually have the film in front of me—I would have it in my hands. But with this equipment, the film itself is not actually there. It is digitized and put onto floppy disks and stored on towers, and you bring up images by pressing buttons." Despite its inherently nontactile nature, the electronic system offered many advantages, the most obvious of which was speed. "As a director, I found it extremely helpful to be able to see a whole series of takes cut in instantly," Marshall noted. "I could review the takes right then and there, without having to wait for the film to be assembled. With this system I could say, 'I have an idea; let's try this,' and I could immediately see if my idea worked or it didn't."

One of the major concerns of the editing process was the seamless intercutting of footage that had been shot in a variety of locales, including interior soundstages, the Costa Rican jungle, and locations throughout Southern California and Africa. Marshall had relied heavily on director of photography Allen Daviau and production designer J. Michael Riva to maintain the continuity of the film's look from one location to another, and their ultimate success eased the burden of matching the footage in editing. "We had a real mosaic of footage to work with," Marshall noted. "But Allen and Michael had done their jobs so well, when we got to editing the film we found that all the footage blended together beautifully. In any one scene we might go from two shots in Africa to a shot in San Bernardino, then to a shot on the stage, and finally to a shot in Simi Valley—and it would all look like Africa."

Another important consideration in the editing of the film was determining which takes best captured the performances of Amy and the gray gorillas. The editing of Amy's scenes was an especially judicious process since she was a featured player in most of the movie. "It was something like cutting scenes featuring a child," said Coates. "We had to pick out the best performance moments, and the moments when she looked most convincing. It was quite tricky. Fortunately, I'd had experience with this kind of thing because I cut *Greystoke*. For *Congo*, we cut in the best Amy bits, the ones that worked the best dramatically, and if there was anything that didn't look quite right, we cut around that. Frank was very conscious of Amy and the grays, and when they looked their best and when they didn't. It was obviously very much to the good of the film that they look as real as possible—and they did."

Starting with a rough cut that was approximately two and a half hours long, Marshall and Coates eventually streamlined the film to two fast-paced hours. "When you get to the editing process," Marshall explained, "you find you don't really need certain shots in the movie. Sometimes it is difficult to let them go, just because *you* know everything you went through to get them. But, inevitably, there are shots that are extraneous. A movie takes on its own life when you finally put it together. In fact, it seems to me that you really make three different movies. There is the movie in preproduction when you are writing and creating the vision. Then it becomes another movie when you are shooting because of certain compromises you have to make due to weather and location and all the variables that come up during production. Finally, the movie takes on another life in postproduction when you realize you don't need that shot and you don't need that scene. By the time editing was completed, *Congo* was a different movie than what it had been in the writing phase or the shooting phase."

Another essential element of postproduction was the incorporation into the film of a final sound mix. Sound mixer Ron Judkins was responsible for the recording of the on-set sound, while Gregg Baxter and Wylie Stateman of Soundelux oversaw, respectively, the looping of dialogue and the creation of sound effects in postproduction. Judkins's recording of a clean sound track on the set had been complicated by the mechanical noise of the servo motors inside Amy's animatronic head. To surmount the problem of sound tracks ruined by the mechanical hum, Baxter was faced with looping many of Amy's scenes, a process in which the actors re-record specific lines of dialogue in a sound studio to replace the original marred sound track.

"I'm not a big fan of looping," Marshall admitted, "and I think it should be used only when it is absolutely necessary. I much prefer using the original dialogue. The performances are better there on the set than they are two months later. Because of that, I only used looping when I absolutely had to. Fortunately, the sound was recorded digitally, so Gregg was able to go in and clean a lot of it up after the fact. An airplane might have gone by during a particular shot, for example, and if the sound of that plane was on a certain frequency, Gregg could go in and take that frequency out. There are always little problems like that to deal with when you are shooting outdoors. But we were able to

Ron Judkins, production sound mixer (l.), and Ian Kelly, video playback. Scenes were simultaneously shot on video through a tap on the movie camera. This way, the scenes could be viewed immediately and reshot if necessary.

do without too much looping because Ron did a great job during production. I had top-of-the-line sound crews all the way from production through postproduction."

Among the sound effects required for *Congo* were Amy's electronic voice, the grays' wheezing language, the rumbling of volcanic and seismic activity for the film's climax, and the distinctive hum of powerful lasers. One of the unknowns going into the sound mix process was what Amy's computer-aided speech should sound like. "We went through a whole casting process to find Amy's voice," Marshall recalled. "We had to decide how the voice should sound—whether she should sound young or old, whether her voice should have some emotion or be completely electronic-sounding. I finally leaned toward her voice having emotion. It still had to sound as if it was coming from a computer; but I thought that the technology we were presenting in the movie was sophisticated enough that it would allow for some real emotional quality in the voice as well. I also decided to go with a young-sounding voice, since Amy is a young gorilla." After listening to a number of actresses, Marshall cast Shayna Fox as the voice of Amy. Soundelux recorded Fox speaking Amy's dialogue, then electronically manipulated the recording to achieve the exact vocal quality Marshall was looking for.

For the wheezing sound of the grays, Marshall had determined that the animalistic "language" should be based on real animal sounds. Soundelux recorded dozens of authentic monkey and gorilla sounds, then processed those recordings electronically to devise a unique sound for the grays that was both frightening and haunting. "You still recognize it as something that comes from an animal," Marshall noted, "but it is also strange and mysterious. The audience hears the sound at the beginning of the film, not realizing what it is. Then the sound recurs at intense moments of the movie."

In some instances, the sound effects added the final punch required to sell a scene. The entire climax of the film, in fact—which included earthquake tremors, Mukenko's fiery eruption, and a laser battle with the grays—would be strategically enhanced and complemented with dynamic sound effects. "We wanted the volcanic eruption and subsequent earthquakes to seem as real and powerful as possible," Marshall explained.

"Unfortunately, most of us who live in Los Angeles are only too aware of what an earthquake really sounds like. I wanted to capture that all-encompassing noise you hear during an earthquake, which sounds as if a train is coming through your living room." Beams emanating from phasic lasers—added in postproduction by ILM—were also given an additional sense of drama with the sound effects. "In reality, a laser gun is a very passive weapon," stated Marshall. "A real laser has no kick to it—it doesn't knock you over, as a powerful gun might do. So I had to find ways to make the laser look like more of an aggressive weapon. One of the ways I did that was through the sound effects. I also directed the actors to react to the lasers as they kicked in—as if they are surprised at how powerful it is."

The final, and perhaps most crucial element of the sound mix to be realized was the music score by Jerry Goldsmith. Goldsmith came to the *Congo* production with more than seventy film scores and nine television program themes to his credit. In a career spanning several decades, the composer had been nominated for Academy Awards more than a dozen times and had been honored with the award for his compelling music score for *The Omen*. Films such as *Seven Days in May, A Patch of Blue, The Sand Pebbles, Planet of the Apes, Patton, Papillon, Chinatown, The Boys from Brazil, Alien, Basic Instinct,* and Kennedy and Marshall's own *Poltergeist* and *Gremlins* had also been scored by Goldsmith.

Because of the intricacies involved in timing the music to specific moments in the film, Goldsmith could not begin composing the score until a final cut of the movie had been locked at the end of March. On March 20, Marshall sat down with Goldsmith to discuss *Congo*'s musical requirements. "My thought was that *Congo* was a big summer movie," Marshall commented, "and that it needed a big, orchestral, popcorn movie score. I also explored with Jerry the idea of incorporating a lot of African instruments and sounds into the score. I wanted it to have a very obvious African flavor, but it also had to be scary and haunting and romantic. One of Jerry's strengths is his ability to create many moods with music. He has scored so many different types of movies, he is a master of coming up with a variety of motifs."

In addition to discussing the general musical style, Marshall

Composer Jerry Goldsmith.

and Goldsmith went through the entire movie looking for those particular moments where music would be required to help create suspense or to drive the story forward. "Music is a tremendous part of the final product," said Marshall. "Steven Spielberg has made the observation that the ending of *E.T.* would have been nothing without John Williams's music. In *Congo*, the score could help to give us romance where we needed it, tension where we needed it; it could sweeten a moment between two characters or add to the hostility. We were able to do all of that, and more, with Jerry's music."

Congo was completed on Memorial Day, 1995. Although approximately two thousand prints of the movie still had to be made and shipped to theaters nationwide in time for the June 9 release, Marshall and his postproduction team had seen the project through to its ultimate conclusion. The score had been completed, visual effects shots from ILM had been cut into the film, and a final sound mix had been achieved. After nearly two years, *Congo* had finally emerged as a cinematic reality.

In the weeks leading up to the release, compelling trailers exhibited in theaters and television ads promoting the movie created an atmosphere of expectation and excitement. Concurrent with the advance publicity campaign for the film was an intense funding and public awareness drive spearheaded by the *Congo* principals and Paramount Pictures to benefit the Dian Fossey Gorilla Fund, an organization which endeavors to study and protect mountain gorillas and their endangered habitat. The filmmakers viewed the tremendous press coverage received by the Foundation as a result of their efforts as a philanthropic and fulfilling complement to the overall *Congo* experience.

With the June 9 release of *Congo,* audiences lined up at theaters across the country. For those audiences, the film was pure entertainment—the kind of exciting adventure movie that is best appreciated on a warm summer night, accompanied by a big, overpriced bag of popcorn. For Marshall, producers Kathleen Kennedy and Sam Mercer, and the hundreds of actors, artists, and camera and construction crew members who contributed to the making of *Congo*, however, the final product was more than just another blockbuster or another impressive credit. Rather, *Congo* represented dedication, commitment, and, for some, a personal sense of achievement. "*Congo* was the hardest thing I have ever done," Frank Marshall commented. "It involved so many extra challenges, so many things you don't normally have to deal with in a movie. In *Alive*, we were on a mountain and it was all right there and every day was the same. In making *Congo*, every day was different, and every day there were a hundred balls to keep in the air. It was the most difficult shoot I've ever been involved with—and I've been in on some pretty grueling shoots.

"Yet *Congo* was also the most rewarding," Marshall continued. "We had a wonderful crew, and we became a family. We worked hard, but we enjoyed each other at the same time. The work involved in making a movie is too hard not to get along in the process. Doing work you enjoy and working with people you like is the most anyone can hope for. In that way, making *Congo* was the ultimate experience."

FROM THE BEST SELLING AUTHOR OF JURASSIC PARK

CONGO

WHERE YOU ARE THE ENDANGERED SPECIES.

PARAMOUNT PICTURES PRESENTS A KENNEDY/MARSHALL PRODUCTION A FILM BY FRANK MARSHALL "CONGO" SPECIAL VISUAL EFFECTS AND ANIMATION BY INDUSTRIAL LIGHT & MAGIC GORILLAS BY STAN WINSTON MUSIC BY JERRY GOLDSMITH EDITED BY ANNE V. COATES, A.C.E. PRODUCTION DESIGNER J. MICHAEL RIVA DIRECTOR OF PHOTOGRAPHY ALLEN DAVIAU, A.S.C. EXECUTIVE PRODUCER FRANK YABLANS BASED ON THE NOVEL BY MICHAEL CRICHTON SCREENPLAY BY JOHN PATRICK SHANLEY PRODUCED BY KATHLEEN KENNEDY AND SAM MERCER DIRECTED BY FRANK MARSHALL

EVERYWHERE JUNE 9

THE KENNEDY/MARSHALL COMPANY